How to Be Lovely

How to Be Lovely

THE AUDREY HEPBURN WAY OF LIFE

Melissa Hellstern

DUTTON

DUTTON
Published by Penguin Group (USA) Inc.
375 Hudson Street, New York, New York 10014, USA
Penguin Books Ltd, Registered Offices: 80 Strand, London WC2R 0RL, England
Penguin Books Australia Ltd, 250 Camberwell Road, Camberwell,
Victoria 3124, Australia
Penguin Books Canada Ltd, 10 Alcorn Avenue, Toronto, Canada M4V 3B2
Penguin Books (NZ) Ltd, Cnr Rosedale and Airborne Roads, Albany,
Aukland 1310, New Zealand

Published by Dutton, a member of Penguin Group (USA) Inc.

First printing, May 2004
20 19 18 17 16 15 14 13 12 11

REGISTERED TRADEMARK—MARCA REGISTRADA

LIBRARY OF CONGRESS CATALOGING-IN-PUBLICATION DATA
Hepburn, Audrey, 1929-
   How to be lovely : the Audrey Hepburn way of life / [compiled and edited] by
Melissa Hellstern.
p. cm.
ISBN 0-525-94823-6
1. Hepburn, Audrey, 1929—Quotations. I. Hellstern, Melissa. II. Title.
PN2287.H43A25 2004
791.4302'8'092—dc22   2003028191

Printed in the United States of America

DESIGNED BY JAYE ZIMET

This book is printed on acid-free paper. ∞

For the two best teachers a girl could ask for

—my grandmothers

Contents

Introduction

When it comes to elegance and style, few women surpass Audrey Hepburn. She has become an adjective—"*so* Audrey"—describing some ethereal combination of grace, elegance, charm, and wisdom.

While her clothing style remains a grounding influence on fashion, it is her character that is certain to withstand the test of time. Audrey taught us that being a woman is as simple as knowing who you are, and who you are not.

And somehow we suspected that if anyone would have the right answers, it would be her: "Amazing the questions they will ask characters like us . . . the questions—all the way from what do I think of love or how does it feel to be a star, to enormous ones, even political, with as many prongs as a pitchfork. Here I am, an innocent little actress trying to do a job, and it seems that my opinion on policy in the Middle East is worth something. I don't say I don't have an opinion, but I doubt it's worth."

To the world, she represented all that a woman could be, and we wanted in. We still do. By looking at her words from interviews over the years, we may just find a new revelation or two, and certainly some we knew all along.

May the light she shared with the world shine on in the lives of those of us she continues to inspire.

"My life isn't theories and formulae.
It's part instinct, part common sense.
Logic is as good a word as any, and I've absorbed what logic
I have from everything and everyone . . . from my mother, from
training as a ballet dancer, from *Vogue* magazine,
from the laws of life and health and nature."

—Audrey Hepburn

How to Find Your Bliss

one
Happiness

"The most important thing is to
enjoy your life—to be happy—
that's all that matters."

A happy life has been pursued in every culture, in every country, in every generation. But after all this time, there are still no rules for how to get it. And the more you try to pin it down, the more elusive it seems.

By now, we surely know that money can't buy it. There are those who have very little and are very happy. And others who seem to have it all, but are not.

Still, we all look for the next reason to be happy. What if it is not about what happens to us, what we own or where we live, but how we look at it? Maybe those rose-colored glasses aren't such a bad idea after all.

"I heard a definition once: Happiness is health and a short memory! I wish I'd invented it, because it is very true."

Attitude Is Everything

Once upon a time, Audrey Hepburn was just a girl.

A girl who took ballet and dreamed of becoming the next Anna Pavlova. Who climbed trees with her brothers. Who read books in her room. Who often felt unsure in the world, but learned to get along. A girl who loved to be loved, just like the rest of us.

As she grew, there were the usual hardships we all find somewhere along the way. Disappointment. Frustration. Struggle. A dwindling bank balance. And some most of us can hardly fathom—overnight success, fame, miscarriages, studio execs, while the whole world watched.

Regardless of what life threw her way, Audrey was a person who sparkled. She never failed to remember what we too often forget—that life itself is a glorious opportunity.

"Pick the day. Enjoy it—to the hilt. The day as it comes. People as they come. . . . The past, I think, has helped me appreciate the present—and I don't want to spoil any of it by fretting about the future."

"Not to live for the day, that would be materialistic—but to treasure the day. I realize that most of us live on the skin—on the surface—without appreciating just how wonderful it is simply to be alive at all."

"My own life has been much more than a fairy tale. I've had my share of difficult moments, but whatever difficulties I've gone through, I've always gotten a prize at the end."

"If my world were to cave in tomorrow, I would look back on all the pleasures, excitements and worthwhilenesses I have been lucky enough to have had. Not the sadnesses, not my miscarriages or my father leaving home, but the joy of everything else. It will have been enough."

> **"But what is happiness except the simple harmony between man and the life he lives?"**
>
> **—Albert Camus**

Listen to Your Mother

Audrey's mother, born Baroness Ella van Heemstra, grew up "wanting more than anything else to be English, slim, and an actress," but her aristocratic heritage prevented such foolishness. Marriage and motherhood were on her agenda.

The Baroness, as she preferred to be called, did marry. She also divorced because, as her friend so aptly put it, "she preferred that to taking a lover, like most." Divorce was hardly commonplace, yet she stood tall as the single mother of two boys, Alexander and Ian.

Just a year later, she married Joseph Hepburn-Ruston. Together, they brought Audrey into the world. But it would be up to her mother to help her navigate through it.

"I could always hear my mother's voice saying, 'Be on time,' and 'Remember to think of others first,' and 'Don't talk a lot about yourself. You are not interesting. It's the others that matter.'"

"Being the daughter of a baroness doesn't make you any different, except that my mother was born in 1900 and had had herself a very strict, Victorian upbringing, if you like. So, she was very demanding of us—of me and my brothers. 'Manners,' as she would say, 'don't forget, are kindnesses. You must always be kind.' Opening the door for old ladies is just a routine so that you know she's helped. And she was always very adamant about that."

"My mother taught me to stand straight, sit erect, use discipline with wine and sweets and to smoke only six cigarettes a day."

"I was given an outlook on life by my mother. . . . It was frowned upon not to think of others first. It was frowned upon not to be disciplined."

"It's that wonderful old-fashioned idea that others come first and you come second. This was the whole ethic by which I was brought up. Others matter more than you do, so don't fuss, dear; get on with it."

"As a child, I was taught that it was bad manners to bring attention to yourself, and to never, ever make a spectacle of yourself. . . . All of which I've earned a living doing."

"I can really take no credit for any talent that Audrey may have. If it's real talent, it's God-given. I might as well be proud of a blue sky, or the paintings in the Flemish exhibition at the Royal Academy."

—her mother, Baroness Ella van Heemstra Hepburn-Ruston

Keep It All in Perspective

Ten-year-old Audrey was just feeling settled at her boarding school outside London when her mother packed up the family and moved to Arnhem, Holland. World War II was coming and only among her own neutral Dutch would her mother, now a single parent, feel safe. "Famous last words," Audrey would later say.

Just days after Audrey's eleventh birthday, the Germans stormed into town. In the years that followed, food and liberty became scarce and treachery lurked everywhere. Audrey would lose friends, uncles, and nearly both brothers.

"Had we known we were going to be occupied for five years, we might have all shot ourselves. We thought it would be over next week . . . six months . . . next year . . . That's how we got through."

When liberation did come—on Audrey's sixteenth birthday—the family had escaped with their lives, but the memories would last a lifetime.

"Don't discount anything awful you hear or read about the Nazis. It's worse than you could ever imagine."

"We lost everything, of course—our houses, our possessions, our money. But we didn't give a hoot. We got through with our lives, which was all that mattered."

> **"At times like this, you learn about death, privation, danger, which makes you appreciate safety and how quickly it can change. You learn to be serious about what counts."**

"Being without food, fearful for one's life, the bombings—all made me appreciative of safety, of liberty. In that sense, the bad experiences have become a positive in my life."

"It made me resilient and terribly appreciative for everything good that came afterward. I felt enormous respect for food, freedom, for good health and family—for human life."

The Two Hepburns

When Audrey came on the scene, Katharine was well-established as an actress and a femme fatale. The studio wasn't sure if there was room for two Hepburns in Hollywood, but Audrey quickly replied, "If you want me, you'll have to take my name too."

It wasn't long before Hollywood mogul Sam Goldwyn was saying, "She's the most exciting thing to hit Hollywood since Garbo and her namesake Katharine."

With different personalities and similar talents, Katharine and Audrey reigned as the queen and the princess of the cinema. To this day, Katharine remains the only woman ever to win four Academy Awards. Remarkably, her first and last Oscars came 48 years apart.

"After so many drive-in waitresses becoming movie stars—it has been a real drought—here is class, somebody who actually went to school, can spell, and possibly play the piano. [Audrey] may be a wispy, thin little thing, but you're really in the presence of something when you see that girl.... That's the element people have or don't have.... She started something new, she started something classy. She, and the other Hepburn, Katharine."

—Billy Wilder

"You see these big brown eyes and that little nose, somebody who looks very vulnerable and crushable, but who has such a sense of rightness that she will challenge people who are failing in a certain way. Katharine Hepburn has the same quality, though hers is much more steak and ice cream, fresh air, open windows, eight hours' sleep. Audrey has a more European grace and elegance."

—Christopher Reeve

Expect Less

By the age of sixteen, Audrey knew much more than most. She had already seen the worst mankind had to offer.

Audrey noticed that during the war people were kind and generous. But once the liberation came, not everyone had learned the lesson. How easily we are able to forget what really matters when it comes down to it.

Audrey always knew just what she wanted in life: safety, food, and family. The rest was just icing on the cake.

What She Said

"Being an actress just happened; I had no intention of it."

"I've had so much more than I ever dreamed possible out of life—[no] great disappointments or hopes that didn't work out . . . I've accomplished far more than I ever hoped to, and most of the time it happened without my seeking it."

"I didn't expect anything
much and because of that
I'm the least bitter woman
I know."

"If I blow my nose, it
gets written all over the
world. But the whole
image people see of me
is on the outside.
Only we ourselves
know what really
goes on; the rest is
all in people's minds."

Be Perfectly Human

Most of us never really knew Audrey. We knew Princess Anne, Holly Golightly, and Eliza Doolittle. In some ways, we made her into the ideal we all wanted her to be—perfect. An image that can be hard to live up to.

Audrey was one of us. She was as real as the girl next door, only smarter.

...t She Said

"Truly, I've never been concerned with any public image. It would drive me around the bend if I worried about the pedestal others have put me on. And also I don't believe it."

"People seem to have this fixed image of me. In a way I think it's very sweet, but it's also a little sad. After all, I'm a human being. When I get angry, I sometimes swear."

CHARADE

"Cary and I had never met before we did *Charade*, so there we all were in Paris, about to have dinner at some terribly smart bistro. As it was early spring, Cary, who always dressed impeccably, was wearing an exquisite light-tan suit. I know I was thrilled to meet him, and I must have been terribly excited, because not ten seconds after we started chatting I made some gesture with my hand and managed to knock an entire bottle of red wine all over poor Cary and his beautiful suit. He remained cool. I, on the other hand, was horrified. Here we'd only just been introduced! If I somehow could have managed to crawl under the table and escape without ever having to see him again, I happily would have."

Live Without Regret

For years, Audrey tried to balance her need for family with the world's need to watch her onscreen, until one day she finally left movie-making behind altogether.

It was during the filming of *Wait Until Dark*, for which she would earn her fifth Oscar nomination, that it hit her. The long separation from her son Sean, now seven years old and in school, was just too much. She had to make a change.

And change she did. In just under two years, she divorced, remarried, and gave birth to her second son, Luca. She also left Hollywood for home, not to be seen again on the big screen for close to ten years. It was the best decision she ever made.

"What would be awful would be to die and look back miserably—seeing only the bad things, the opportunities missed, or what could have been."

"It would be terribly sad, wouldn't it, to look back on your life in films and not know your children? For me there's nothing more pleasant or exciting or lovely or rewarding than seeing my children grow up . . . and they only grow up once, remember."

"You can only hope to get a combination of happy work and a happy life."

"One thing I would have dreaded would be to look back on my life and only have movies."

"I never expected to be a star, never counted on it, never even wanted it. Not that I didn't enjoy it all when it happened. (But) it's not as if I were a great actress. I'm not Bergman. I don't regret for a minute making the decision to quit movies for my children."

"I may not always be offered work, but I'll always have my family."

"She had trouble having children, so when she had Sean, she felt that God had bestowed grace upon her. After she had Luca, she didn't feel like working much. 'Life is too short,' she said."

—Hubert de Givenchy

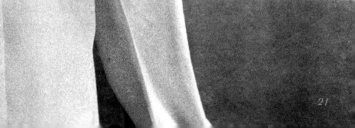

How to Make Your Mark

Success

"Success is like reaching an
important birthday and finding
out you're exactly the same.
All I feel is a responsibility to live
up to it. And even, with luck,
survive it."

No matter what profession you have chosen in the world—singer, banker, dry cleaner, homemaker, lawyer, or goat herder—chances are you are doing it for one of two reasons: for love or for money.

At some point, even the diehard optimists among us are forced to choose between being left starved for affirmation, or, say, food on the table. Yet whether you get up every morning and don a classic navy three-button suit or just a bathrobe, one thing is certain: You want to be a success.

"When I was a child, I didn't even
comprehend the meaning of the
words 'film star.'"

Be a Good Student

Audrey began her serious study of ballet at twelve. During World War II, dancing was a welcome distraction. She earned a dime per lesson teaching small classes of her own, working a gramophone wound by hand. In darkened basements, she danced in fundraisers for the Resistance, where applause was too dangerous a risk.

Dance led her to Amsterdam after the war and eventually to the famed Rambert School of Ballet in west London.

Though Audrey was praised for her magnetic quality and single-minded determination, what she needed most was money. Enter musical reviews, modeling assignments, and bit parts in movies. Little did she know, directors of stage and screen would soon follow.

While she would not fulfill her dream "to wear a tutu and dance at Covent Garden," it would be through dance that she would learn all she needed to know about how to succeed.

"Winja was the first [dancer] I really got to know and could call a friend. She was a beautiful world-class dancer [and she] helped this very young girl in Arnhem believe that she could become one too."

—AH on her ballet teacher Winja Marova

"The work ethic—don't complain, don't give in even if you're tired, don't go out the night before you have to dance. Sonia taught me that if you really worked hard, you'd succeed, and that everything has to come from the inside."

—AH on her ballet teacher Sonia Gaskell

"Dancers do a lot of technical things out of good habit. When we relax we never get sloppy. In my case that's because when my ballet teacher, Madame Rambert, would catch us folding our arms or slouching our shoulders, she'd give us a good rap across the knuckles with a stick. . . . Dancers learn to feel when their posture is not graceful."

—AH on her ballet teacher Madame Marie Rambert

"Success is liking yourself, liking what you do, and liking how you do it."

—Maya Angelou

When Opportunity Knocks, Answer

At just twenty-one, Audrey was in London working in musicals and cabaret shows. She took modeling assignments and bit parts in movies, but only for the easy extra cash. In the world of dance, movies and modeling were not taken very seriously.

And then lightning struck. Twice.

Audrey was on location filming *Monte Carlo Baby*. Her role: a movie star. The French playwright Sidonie-Gabrielle Colette saw her and famously exclaimed, "Voila! My Gigi!" Suddenly she was moving to New York to star on Broadway.

But before her bags were packed, her screen test reached acclaimed director William Wyler, who decided to make her a princess in *Roman Holiday*. A little over a year later, so did the rest of the world.

"My career is a complete mystery to me. It's been a total surprise since the first day. I never thought I was going to be an actress, I never thought I was going to be in movies, I never thought it would all happen the way it did."

"I was hoping to be a ballet dancer and I've studied the best I could. . . . And that went on as long as, you know, I could. But you do finally need some money to buy ballet shoes and go to the dentist, so I got a job in a musical. And then I got a little part in a movie."

"William Wyler came to London looking for an unknown, and I was fully qualified."

"I tried to explain to all of them that I wasn't ready to do a lead, but they didn't agree, and I certainly wasn't going to argue with them."

"Opportunities don't often come along. So, when they do, you have to grab them."

"This is how I got into movies: not because I thought it was so wonderful to be in one and, gosh, here's my dream coming true, but because I need money to live. And so, when another opportunity was offered me, I took it. Gratefully."

GIGI

"I had a part in a movie and a scene was being shot in the Hotel de Paris in Monte Carlo. [Collette] was staying there and it coincided with her search for an unknown to play Gigi. And that's how it all happened. I met her and I did tell her I couldn't possibly do a play, because I had never done a play before and what a crazy thing to say . . . but she said 'Well, you're a dancer. You know how to work hard. You know, 'get on with it.' So off I went to New York and did *Gigi*."

Wing It If You Have To

In the chorus line, Audrey always got noticed. Everyone who met her saw it. That je ne sais quoi; that elusive special something. Everyone but Audrey.

Now she had become the first actress in history simultaneously signed to star in a Broadway play and a Hollywood movie. But Audrey was never one to take to the stage unprepared and here they were, asking her to do just that.

Despite waning confidence and major performance anxiety, Audrey gave it her all and took the chance.

"I am not an actress. You will regret it."

"I was asked to act when I really couldn't; I was asked to sing *Funny Face* when I couldn't sing, and to dance with Fred Astaire when I couldn't dance, and do all kinds of things I was neither expecting nor prepared for; all I had to do then was learn how to cope with the results."

"I never really became an actress—in the sense that when people ask me how I did it, my only answer is 'I wouldn't know.' I just walked on the set knowing my lines and took it from there."

"I act the same way now as I did forty years ago: I was never backed up by professional training, had no Shakespeare at school, none of that. I had to skip it all and do it with feeling instead of technique."

"All my life I've been in situations where I've had no technique, but if you feel enough, you can get away with murder."

"I've never believed in this God-given talent. I adored my work and I did my best."

Work Hard

Audrey survived the Nazis and her ballet teachers, but when it came to acting, she often wondered if she would make it. In place of doubt came diligence.

At the end of the day, when the director yelled "Cut!" or the curtain fell, she just knew she did the best she could.

What She Said

"If you want to get psychological, you can say my definiteness stems from underlying feelings of insecurity and inferiority. I couldn't conquer these feelings by acting indecisive. I found the only way to get the better of them was by putting my foot down, by adopting a forceful and concentrated drive."

"I was not an actress when I came to movies. I was a dancer. So, I had no experience. I had experience in working, working hard. Ballet is hard. Discipline. Those were the things I could contribute."

"I had incredible luck. But I was not an overnight story. My mother and I lived in one room in London. I had no money and worked for eight years as a total unknown, hoofing my way through dance shows, television and bits in movies . . . I'd acted so very little. I'd had no training, no preparation. But I'd been working many, many years before that 'magical' 120 minutes happened."

"I fell into this career. I was unknown, insecure, inexperienced, and skinny. I worked very hard—that I'll take credit for—but I don't understand any of it."

"To follow, without halt, one aim: There's the secret of success."

—Anna Pavlova

FUNNY FACE

"I never saw anyone work so hard. She was tireless in learning both the songs and the dances. It wasn't like Cyd Charisse or Ginger Rogers, who did it all the time. Roger Edens would say, 'Audrey, take tomorrow off. You've been working sixteen hours a day.' She'd say, 'No, I'll be here at nine.' And then she'd be there at eight."

—Leonard Gershe,
SCREENWRITER

LOVE IN THE AFTERNOON

"I have been in pictures for thirty years, and I have never had a more enthusiastic leading lady than Audrey. She puts more life and energy into her acting than anyone else I've ever met."

—Gary Cooper

Nerves Are Normal

Two projects into her American career and already Audrey was the love of the land. Reporters and critics alike were smitten, writing glowing love letters in adulation. Fans hung on her every word, clamoring to unravel a bit of the mystery. Soon enough, her fellow actors followed suit.

Audrey became only the second actress to win a Tony award, for *Ondine*, and an Oscar, for *Roman Holiday*, in the same year (actually, in the same month). Her first forays—both onstage and on screen—as a leading lady.

"I lack self-confidence. I don't know whether I shall ever get it. Perhaps it is better to be unsure of yourself, as I am. But it is very tiring."

The academy would later nominate her for *Sabrina*, *The Nun's Story*, *Breakfast at Tiffany's* and *Wait Until Dark*. But no amount of public adoration could fill the void she felt on the inside. When it came to acting, Audrey would never feel completely confident.

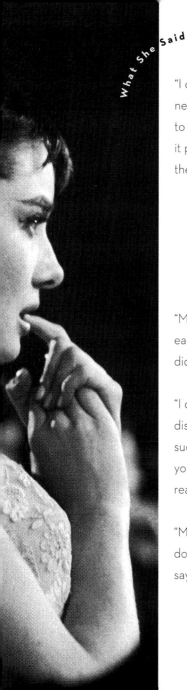

"I came to work every day . . . terribly nervous . . . terribly insecure, was I going to get the words right, was I going to do it properly? And, oh, the relief when they said, 'Print.' "

"There is a Dutch saying, 'Don't fret; it will happen differently anyway.' I believe that."

"My confidence came and went with each movie; once I'd finished one, I didn't know if I'd ever work again."

"I don't think your insecurity ever disappears. Sometimes I think the more successful you become, the less secure you feel. This is kind of frightening, really."

"My epithet will be, 'It's nerves what done her in,' as Eliza Doolittle would say."

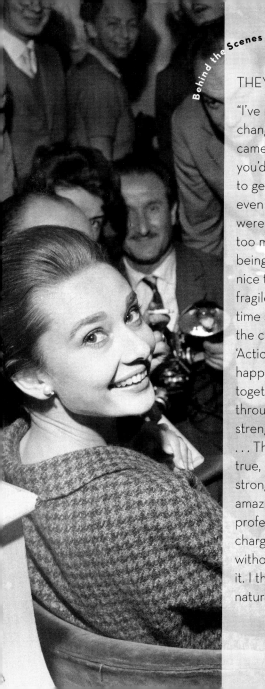

THEY ALL LAUGHED

"I've never seen anybody change so much in front of a camera as Audrey. In life, you'd think, 'How is she going to get through the day or even the hour?' Her hands were shaking, she's smoking too much, she's worried, she's being kind of desperately nice to everybody, she's so fragile . . . But between the time she stepped in front of the camera and you said 'Action!,' something happened. She pulled it together. A kind of strength through vulnerability—strength like an iron butterfly . . . The performance was true, never weak, always strong and clear. It was an amazing thing to watch, this professional completely in charge of her instrument without even thinking about it. I think it was all second nature."

—Peter Bogdanovich

Use Whatever Tools Necessary

Audrey never publicly subscribed to any of the popular acting theories. The Stanislavsky Method taught us that, to act, one must emotionally feel what is needed, one must take his or her own personality to the stage. Audrey would embody this "believable truth" effortlessly.

The Method didn't give her what she needed. She knew plenty. In the absence of confidence, Audrey found the right clothes. In the absence of technique, Audrey found her own way.

"Clothes, *per se*, the costume is terribly important to me, always has been. Perhaps because I didn't have any technique for acting when I started because I had never learned to act. I had a sort of make-believe, like children do."

"It has always been a difficulty to perform. How I get around it is, I'm not Audrey Hepburn. I'm Holly Golightly or Eliza Doolittle."

"What has always helped me a great deal, for instance, are the clothes, because as I didn't have this technique of being able to deal with a part in, you know, however way it was, it was often an enormous help to know that you looked the part. Then the rest wasn't so tough anymore."

"In a very obvious way, let's say you do a period picture, whether it was *War and Peace*, or *The Nun's Story*, where you wear a habit. Once you're in that habit of that nun, it's not that you become a nun. But you walk differently, you feel something."

"Those movies were fairy tales. That's always been me . . . I've never changed. A princess or a flower girl were all parts of me and I was parts of them."

MY FAIR LADY

"In that absolutely sublime dress, with my hair dressed to kill, and diamonds everywhere, I felt super! All I had to do was walk down the staircase in Professor Higgins' house, but the dress made me do it. Clothes, like they say, make the man, but in my case, they also gave me the confidence I often needed."

Be Prepared to Sacrifice

The American press was instantly enthralled with Audrey. But it was James Hanson, eventually Lord Hanson, who found her first. Heir to a British transport fortune and a fun-loving playboy, one day he proposed. Audrey said yes, without hesitation.

While they were dating, Audrey found Broadway and stardom found her. Ever hopeful, the couple pressed forward. Invitations were sent out, the wedding party enlisted.

Some say the studio admonished her for going through with it. Certainly the work was hard and getting harder. Regardless, Audrey called things off before *Roman Holiday* hit the theaters.

It wouldn't be the only relationship to suffer the burns of limelight, just the first.

INTERVIEWER: What quality brought you fame?

AH: Learning to do without things.

INTERVIEWER: Such as?

AH: Marriage, for instance.

"The business of running a house is a full-time job. What happens if I've been so busy cooking my husband's supper that I don't know my lines at rehearsal next day? I lose my job—and probably lose my husband too."

"My greatest ambition is to have a career without becoming a career woman."

"When I couldn't find time to attend to the furnishing of our London flat, I suddenly knew I'd make a pretty bad wife . . . making him stand by, holding my coat, while I signed autographs."

How to Be Beautiful

three

Health

"Look, whenever I hear or read
I'm beautiful, I simply don't
understand it . . . I'm certainly not
beautiful in any conventional way.
I didn't make my career on
beauty."

Our youth-obsessed, weight-obsessed culture leaves us feeling pretty ugly indeed. Most of us are on a mission to turn back the hands of time. It's like staying alive longer has somehow lost its appeal.

To evaporate fat, remove wrinkles, and rid our thighs of cellulite, we fill our grocery carts with diet supplements, food substitutes, creams and potions. We cram in workouts where meals used to be. We stay up late watching home fitness equipment dramatically change lives.

Nevertheless, age happens. And all that time we spend trying to stop it only gives us less time to reap the benefits—actually enjoying life.

Being young is one thing, but healthy is beautiful at any age.

"The cities are not a place for you if you are famous."

Beware the City Life

As Audrey catapulted to stardom, she completed two Broadway plays and two motion pictures in only three years. She worked hard. She answered all the questions. And she learned just what it meant to be a star: exhaustion. At just twenty-five, Audrey needed a rest.

Enter Switzerland. The mountains, the quiet, the fresh air. It was everything she could possibly want, and it always would be.

Audrey spent a lot of time in the big cities: London, Paris, New York, Los Angeles, and Rome, just to name a few, but the city would never be her place.

Audrey's Guilty Pleasures

One of Audrey's earliest onscreen lines was: "Who wants a ciggy?" She would go on to smoke in *Roman Holiday*, *Breakfast at Tiffany's*, *Charade*, *How to Steal a Million*, *Paris When It Sizzles* and *Two for the Road*.

The British brand Wills' Gold Flake was her brand of choice (until they were taken off the market for high tar content) and later Kents. Audrey knew the dangers of smoking, so she often tried to cut down, but never managed to stop altogether. More often than not, her habit increased in times of stress.

In the evenings, Audrey was known to ask, "Would you be very shocked if I poured myself a small whisky? It's awfully early, I know, but it must be six o'clock somewhere in the world." How could anyone deny her? Maybe that's why the Rat Pack labeled her "The Princess."

People magazine gave us a whole new perspective: "The day typically wound down with Hepburn ambling around the house with a Kent cigarette and her nightly 'two fingers' of J&B Scotch."

It was Elizabeth Taylor who said: "The problem with people who have no vices is that generally you can be pretty sure they're going to have some pretty annoying virtues." It's no wonder she and Audrey were good friends.

"She's the kind of girl you know Mother would love, the kind they built best selling musicals around."

—Frank Sinatra

"I'm not a city person . . . I'm very bored by cement."

"In the city, one tries to live as though one were on a farm—that is, naturally: You try to exercise, but you can't always; you eat the things that are good for you, but you also eat things that are not good for you."

"Besides, there is something about society and life in the city that oppresses me, a procedure of obliteration. The air is polluted, the backfire of cars is reminiscent of guns, and the noise is so bad you can't hear properly."

"If I had lived in London or New York or Hollywood, it would have been outlandish. I never liked the city. I always wanted the countryside."

Relax

Time and time again, journalists asked for Audrey's beauty secrets. Women the world over clamored to find the products, the regimen, the tools that might make them a bit more like her.

Little did they realize, they weren't secrets at all, just good common sense.

"You have to be as relaxed as possible about food and fitness and the rest of it, or you'll be a slave to your beauty habits . . . You may have great skin, but you'll become a robot."

"I'm not one who has rules. I am not a person who must have so many hours sleep so that my skin will look good. I love to walk, so I do get lots of air . . . lots and lots of oxygen. And I sleep marvelously well. I need eight or nine hours to make me completely happy; otherwise I long for a nap. But if I don't have one, it doesn't destroy me. I'm very relaxed and unmethodical about myself. I do what I have to do and let it go at that."

Eat Well

Through pregnancies and heartaches, Audrey remained her perfectly thin self. Nearly five foot seven, and just one hundred ten pounds.

At home, Audrey ate simply. Fresh foods. Lots of fruits and vegetables. Not too many sauces. Enough protein (after all, protein is important to a dancer), but not too much as she got older. Nothing too heavy. Nothing that would slow her down.

Healthy choices and darn good genes kept Audrey thin, but she ate plenty.

"When you have had the strength to survive starvation, you never again send back a steak simply because it's under-done."

"I seem to have a sort of built-in leveler. I've a tremendously good appetite—I eat everything, everything—but as soon as I'm satisfied, a little hatch closes and I stop."

"I eat very well and I eat everything I want."

"I don't put on weight—it's not part of my metabolism. I was just born this way."

"I'm not a snacker. But I eat awfully well at meals and all the things I like."

"Audrey would come to my house and we'd have pasta and vanilla ice cream and fudge sauce. That was our great treat."

—Doris Brynner,
CLOSE FRIEND

"I know some people who eat nothing but salad and vinegar. But not her. She was always eating spaghetti or a version of it."

—Audrey Wilder,
CLOSE FRIEND

BREAKFAST AT TIFFANY'S

"I remember ... Audrey's horror over my guzzling the hot donut my hairdresser brought to the studio at crack of dawn, while she broke out one tragic bran muffin and the thermos of Tiger's Milk ... then Audrey instantly giving up her muffin to reform a fallen sister. An act of utmost sweetness because it deprived her of—and heaven knows she needed it!—even mini-nourishment."

—Dana Wynter

Run with the Dogs

Audrey would lavish attention on many animals over the years—cats, a donkey, doves, canaries, and even a fawn named Ip. But it was dogs that she loved best. "My little hamburgers," she called them.

The notables include Mr. Famous (Famey to his friends), who became a fixture on movie sets and even garnered the attention of photographer Richard Avedon. Then, after a tragic moment on Wilshire Boulevard, there was Assam of Assam. Sam was a replacement, but a nice one.

In her later years, there would be Jack Russells— five of them: Missy, Tuppy, Penny, Piceri, and Jackie. Leave it to Audrey to love the high-strung kind.

"Prized possession: My dogs. I'm potty about them."

"Who thinks you're as fantastic as your dog does?"

"I walk with my dogs which keeps me fit. I talk to my dogs, which keeps me sane. I can't think of anything that makes one happier than to cuddle and play and start the day with a warm puppy."

"I think an animal, especially a dog, is possibly the purest experience you can have. They are totally dependent on you, and therefore completely vulnerable."

GREEN MANSIONS

"For the past few weeks she had been living with a very young fawn. . . . Ip, as the fawn was called, would come right up and lie down next to her when she was having a nap. They were literally in touch, something I had never seen between a human being and a forest animal."

—Bob Willoughby
PHOTOGRAPHER

Grow Something

Audrey had long been an early riser. Just as the sun began to warm the hills, she could often be found in the crisp Swiss morning air of her garden.

Flowers and Audrey went together naturally. In her last film project, Audrey traveled extensively to explore the secret rhythmic cadence of flowers and the colorful language of nature as the host of the Emmy Award–winning documentary series *Gardens of the World*.

But it was always the gardens at home that gave her the most joy. If home was her sanctuary, the garden was surely her altar.

What She Said

"I'm grateful for everything that's green. When I didn't have a dime, I held to the dream of one day having my own orchard with fruit trees and a place to grow vegetables."

"Well, it's all about the same thing, isn't it? Children and flowers, it's life, it's survival . . . I think that's what life is all about actually—about children and flowers."

Get Plenty of Vitamin C

There was no cake to mark Audrey's sixteenth birthday. By the fifth year of the occupation, milk, butter, eggs, and sugar were scarce indeed. Of course, so was most everything else. But on that day, the day of liberation, a soldier gave her a handful of chocolate bars in celebration: "I ate all of them and got sick."

Forever after, chocolate was one of the few things that Audrey could not do without. That creamy luxury was always proof that in the end, life was a sweet proposition.

What She Said

"We talked about food endlessly—what meal we would eat when the war was over. I think mine was chocolate cake."

"Let's face it, a nice creamy chocolate cake does a lot for a lot of people; it does for me."

Be a Realist

Upon Audrey's death, an editorial in *The New York Times* would best express what we could not yet put into words:

"Nearly forty years later Audrey Hepburn's face was that of someone who'd squinted into the sun, laughed a few laughs, shed a few tears. The forehead showed some wrinkles, the eyes showed some more, and the strong jawline was softening around the edges.

As unwilling to fake youth as she had been to fake voluptuousness, she looked like the 63-year-old woman she was. Which is to say, better than any 63-year-old woman who's pretending that she isn't. Would that she were going to be around longer, to teach us all how to grow old."

INTERVIEWER: Can a woman age in a beautiful and interesting way?

AH: We've got to believe that! Otherwise, what would you do— shoot yourself?

"As the years go on, you see changes in yourself, but you've got to face that—everyone goes through it . . . Either you have to face up to it and tell yourself you're not going to be eighteen all your life, or be prepared for a terrible shock when you see the wrinkles and white hair."

"(Getting older) doesn't frighten me, but I wish I didn't have to, because I like life a lot . . . But certainly I try to keep young-looking. I have a woman's vanity about that."

"You know, one would love to be younger, to have more time. Yet, there's a big advantage in being older . . . It's an excuse in a way to get rid of a lot of the tension you have when you are young . . . if I were twenty years old, I doubt I'd be able to say that so serenely since I'd have to get out and prove things to myself, make a living and still see the world. I couldn't just relax under my apple tree in Switzerland."

"I don't want to be a perennial teenager."

How to Get What You Deserve

four
Love

"We all want to be loved, don't
we? Everyone looks for a way of
finding love. It's a constant search
for affection in every walk of life."

*Y*es, love (no, no, not money) makes the world go round. Coupling is good for our mental and physical health, our sex lives, and our bank accounts. It gives us legitimacy, a place to fit inside the larger whole.

But if you aren't a grownup when you say "I do," chances are you will be soon. Sharing in-laws, money, housework, and careers will either help you to grow, or it will break you apart.

Romantic love challenges us to become whole the way nothing else will. We go into it thinking we'll learn about another person, secretly hoping for their stamp of approval.

Instead, we end up learning the most about ourselves.

"What can one learn about them? They're human beings, with all the frailties that women have; I think they're more vulnerable than women. I really do. You can hurt a man so easily."

Be Willing to Get Hurt

Though some of it was heavier than most, Audrey had baggage just like everybody else. She was a child of divorce, a child of war.

Still, when Audrey loved, she did so without reservation. She gave her whole heart. Despite some disappointments and heartaches along the way—miscarriages, failed marriages, and lost love—it would prove worth the risk.

"Sabrina was a dreamer who lived a fairy-tale, and she was a romantic, an incorrigible romantic, which I am. I could never be cynical. I wouldn't dare. I'd roll over and die before that."

"Love does not terrify me. But the going away of it does. I have been made terribly aware of how everything can be wrenched away from you and your life torn apart. If I had known very secure nights all my life, if I had never seen or felt the fear of being tortured or deported or blown up into a million pieces, then I would not fear it."

"It has stayed with me through my own relationships. When I fell in love and got married, I lived in constant fear of being left. Whatever you love most, you fear you might lose, you know it can change. Why do you look from left to right when you cross the street? Because you don't want to get run over. But, you still cross the street."

"The best thing to hold on to in life is each other."

"I let my heart get the better of me. I often let my heart get the better of me!"

"But I'm a romantic woman. What is there without it?"

TWO FOR THE ROAD

"Playing a love scene with a woman as sexy as Audrey, you sometimes get to the edge where make-believe and reality are blurred, all that staring into each other's eyes—you pick up vibes that are decidedly not fantasy . . . The time spent with Audrey is one of the closest I've ever had."

—Albert Finney

When Flirting, Be Subtle

One thing is certain: When it came to attracting men, Audrey hardly had to work for it.

Many thought it had to do with her eyes, her sense of humor and her vulnerability. Whatever it was, Audrey knew how to use it. Just ask any man she ever met.

"There's never any need for any woman to ogle any man. Ogling only puts the men off. It scares them away. In fact, the faintest flutter of an eyelash should be enough."

"Sex appeal is something that you feel deep down inside. It's suggested rather than shown. I'll admit that I'm not as well-stacked as Sophia Loren or Gina Lollobrigida, but there is more to sex appeal than just measurements."

"Men say women are more jealous. Men are just as jealous if they're in love with women."

BREAKFAST AT TIFFANY'S

HOLLY GOLIGHTLY: I'll tell you one thing, Fred darling, I'd marry you for your money in a minute. Would you marry me for my money?

PAUL VARJAK: In a minute.

HOLLY: Well, I guess it's lucky neither of us is rich, huh?

CHARADE

PETER JOSHUA: Do we know each other?

REGINA LAMPERT: Why, do you think we're going to?

PETER: I don't know, how would I know?

REGINA: Because I already know an awful lot of people, and until one of them dies, I couldn't possibly meet anyone else.

PETER: Hmmmm, well, if anyone goes on the critical list, let me know.

REGINA: Quitter.

"She was so gracious and graceful that everybody fell in love with her after five minutes. Everybody was in love with this girl, I included. My problem was that I am a guy who speaks in his sleep. I toss around and talk and talk. . . . But fortunately, my wife's first name is Audrey as well."

—Billy Wilder

"Audrey knew how to handle flattery when it was not connected with a come-on. Once we were talking, and I kept looking at her until she said, 'What's the matter, what are you looking at?' I said, 'Audrey you're just so beautiful, I can't stand it.' She giggled and took my hand and said, 'Come to dinner.' I said, 'Okay.' It was wonderfully done."

—Andre Previn

"Before I even met Audrey, I had a crush on her, and after I met her, just a day later, I felt as if we were old friends. . . . Most men who worked with her felt both fatherly or brotherly about her, while harboring romantic feelings about her . . . she was the love of my life."

—William Holden

Mind the Male Ego

In 1953, Audrey met Mel Ferrer at a dinner party hosted by Gregory Peck. Though he was twice-divorced, they found much in common. Mel was a writer, a dancer, a singer, a director, a father of four and a humanitarian. He even spoke French.

They starred together on Broadway (Mel's idea, no less) in *Ondine*. During the run of the play, Audrey accepted a Tony for her role and an Oscar for *Roman Holiday*. Their great love helped Audrey immortalize her most memorable characters on screen, but son Sean was their greatest collaboration.

"I met him, liked him, loved him and married him."

Then came *Wait Until Dark*. Mel produced; she made an astounding one million dollars. During filming, both were forced to leave Sean behind to continue his schooling.

Audrey yearned to work less and live more. Not only did she resent the work, but also the husband who kept pushing her to do it. At thirty-nine, Audrey chose to go it alone.

"I thought a marriage between two good, loving people had to last until one of them died. I can't tell you how disillusioned I was."

"I knew how difficult it had to be to be married to a world celebrity, recognized everywhere, usually second-billed on the screen and in real life. How Mel suffered! But, believe me, I put my career second."

"Success isn't so important for a woman, and with the baby I felt I had everything a wife could wish for. But it's not enough for a man. He couldn't live with himself just being Audrey Hepburn's husband."

Know When to Walk Away

In 1968, Audrey and Andrea Dotti cruised the Greek Isles with mutual friends. On the set of *Roman Holiday*, Andrea was a boy of fourteen who had shaken her hand. As a man, he was an Italian psychiatrist, nine years her junior. Somewhere between Ephesus and Athens, they fell in love.

Just after their wedding, Audrey was pregnant. She was ecstatic, but the doctors ordered bed rest, and rest meant Switzerland. While she was away, pictures of infidelity turned up in the papers. Audrey did her best to look the other way.

She soon returned to Rome and embraced her life as an Italian housewife, but home was not enough for Andrea. Audrey retreated to Switzerland more often until kidnapping threats sent her there for good. One day absence no longer made her heart grow fonder. And at fifty-one, she again chose to go it alone.

"Your heart just breaks, that's all. But you can't judge, or point fingers. You just have to be lucky enough to find somebody who appreciates you."

"If there's love, unfaithfulness is impossible. I don't care who it is . . . Those open marriages don't work. An arrangement is possible when both people basically don't love each other anymore."

"Marriage should be only one thing: Two people decide they love each other so much that they want to stay together. Whether they sign a piece of paper or not, it's still a marriage, with a sacred contract of trust and respect. To me, the only reason to be married and stay married is just that . . . So, if in some way I don't fulfill what he needs in a woman emotionally, physically, sexually, or whatever it is—and if he feels he needs somebody else, then I could not stick around. I'm not the kind to stay and make scenes."

"There's a curious thing about pain or hardship. In the beginning, it's an enemy, it's something that you don't want to face or think about or deal with. Yet, with time it becomes almost a friend."

"It was a very strong, complicated relationship. When Audrey started to find out about his infidelity, she said, 'I'm going away.' He said, 'I promise it won't happen again,' and she believed him. She later found out he couldn't be believed, but I think he was genuine when he promised."

—Anna Cataldi,
JOURNALIST

CHARADE

SYLVIE GAUDET: When you start to eat like this, something is the matter.

REGINA LAMBERT: Sylvie, I am getting a divorce.

SYLVIE: What?! From Charles?!

REGINA: He's the only husband I have. I've tried to make it work, really, I have, but . . .

SYLVIE: But what?

REGINA: Oh, I can't explain. It's just that I am too miserable to go on any longer like this.

SYLVIE: It is infuriating that your unhappiness does not turn to fat!

Know What to Look For

When Audrey was a young girl of eleven waiting out the war in Arnhem, Holland, a four-year-old boy, Robert Wolders, also waited in a village not far down the road.

Audrey was reeling from the failure of her second marriage when they finally met at Connie Wald's house. Robert also needed cheering up. His wife, Merle Oberon, had recently lost her battle with cancer. At dinner, they shared their Dutch heritage, their passion for books, and their heartaches.

With time their instant friendship became love. Audrey called Robbie her husband, though they never officially tied the knot. Devotion, she learned, is paperless.

"The kind of man I'm attracted to can be tall or short, fair or dark, handsome or homely. Physical good looks don't necessarily appeal to me just by themselves. If a man has that indefinable quality that I can only call 'warmth' or 'charm,' then I'll feel at ease with him."

"I love Robbie very much. It's no *Romeo and Juliet*; we've had our tiffs, but very few. We're both patient, no huge tempers. It's a wonderful friendship. . . . if there's enough friendship and love, the fame doesn't hurt and you overcome it."

"If it ain't broke, don't fix it!"

"It took me a long time to find someone like him, but sometimes it is better late than never. If I'd met him when I was eighteen, I wouldn't have appreciated him. I would have thought, 'That's the way everyone is.'"

"There is no reason why we shouldn't marry, but we're just very happy the way we are."

"Why bother? It's lovely this way. The idea is, sort of, more romantic. Because it does mean we're together because we want to be. Not because now we have to be. It's a slight difference, but maybe it's a very good one."

"Robert made Audrey so happy. She and I both chose very badly as far as men are concerned, as most actors do, because one doesn't have time to give it a chance. But Robert was wonderful, very European, very genteel—a true gentleman in every way."

—Eva Gabor

"[I asked her] 'How do you and Rob do it? How do you spend all this time together, travel together, live together, without killing each other?' She said, 'We just enjoy going through the world together.' It was the sweetest thing to see their little jokes—that playful, mischievous side of her. She was so smart, so well-read, spoke gazillions of languages. No wonder Robbie never got bored with her."

—Julie Leifermann
PRODUCER

MY FAIR LADY

"You see, Mrs. Higgins, apart from the things one can pick up, the
difference between a lady and a flower girl is not how she
behaves, but how she is treated. I shall always be a flower girl to
Professor Higgins because he always treats me as a flower girl,
and always will. But I know I shall
always be a lady to Colonel
Pickering because he
always treats me as
a lady, and
always will."

—Eliza Doolittle

How to Nurture Those You Love

Family

"Whatever a man might do,
whatever misery or heartache
your children might give you—and
they give you a lot—however much
your parents might irritate you—it
doesn't matter because you
love them."

W hen it comes to family, we are dealt a hand and do our best to play it out. Life is a card game; a lot is left to chance.

We blame our parents for many things: low self-esteem, intimacy issues, a love of onions; until we realize that they are just human beings and no amount of whining will change that. In the end, they did the best they could.

With the never-ending optimism our parents had for us, we may have children of our own. If we are lucky, we manage not to make all the same mistakes. Yet inevitably, we all get caught doing or saying something just like our mother. It is a humbling moment indeed.

"Mother and I are not alike, but we get on awfully well."

Love Your Mother Anyway

The Baroness Ella van Heemstra Hepburn-Ruston was, in many ways, Audrey's greatest champion. Before ballet teachers and directors stepped in—and even after they did—she was pushing Audrey to reach new heights. Of course, not always with the gentlest of hands.

Audrey's mother was not the easiest of women. She kept Audrey at a distance and rarely gave her approval (more often, she added fuel to Audrey's fire of self-doubt). Nevertheless, when stardom came, Ella was very proud. Though the last one she would tell would be Audrey.

"My mother was not an affectionate person. She was a fabulous mother, but she had a Victorian upbringing of great discipline, of great ethics. She was very strict, very demanding of her children. She had a lot of love within her, but she was not always able to show it."

"I am not beautiful. My mother once called me an ugly duckling. But, listed separately, I have a few good features."

"Many years ago, my mother said to me, 'Considering that you have no talent, it's really extraordinary where you've got.' She said it in the middle of all the lovely successes I was having. She wasn't putting me down. She was saying how fortunate I was."

"There were times when I thought she was cold—but she loved me in her heart, and I knew that all along."

"Audrey once told me that she never felt loved by her mother, but Ella did love her, believe me. Often people can't tell the object of their love they love them; they'll tell other people instead. I probably would have hated Ella as a mother. But I loved her as a friend."

—Leonard Gershe,
SCREENWRITER

Forgive Your Father

Audrey had very little relationship with her father. For many years, her last memory of him was when he put her on a bright orange (the Dutch national color) plane bound for Holland. Audrey was just six.

After the war, she learned through the Red Cross that he had moved to Ireland. But it would be something close to a lifetime before she would be brave enough to say, "I want to see you."

After all those years, the reunion was not quite what she had hoped. His heart just wasn't big enough.

"My father leaving left me insecure, for life perhaps. I do think there are things, experiences in childhood, that form you for the rest of your life."

"Having my father cut himself off from me when I was only six was desperately awful. If I could have just seen him regularly, I would have felt he loved me. But as it was, I always envied other people's fathers, came home with tears, because they had a daddy."

"He looked the way I remembered him. Older, yes, but much the same. Slim and tall. He was living in a tiny apartment, just two rooms, but not because he couldn't afford more. It was very hard to find anything bigger in that section of Dublin."

"I think he was proud. My mother was that way, too. My whole family was. It was a job well done, but you didn't make a lot of fuss about it."

"With me, she seemed eager to talk about it and get my feelings, perhaps in part to explain why she could not love her parents as unconditionally as I or others loved theirs. But it didn't wreck her life; it made her more just and fair. Audrey fought the tendencies to reject her parents. She was extremely good to both of them."

—Robert Wolders

Believe in Miracles

On the set of *The Unforgiven*, Audrey was thrown from the gray stallion she rode bareback. She not only broke her back, but soon after she also miscarried. Later she sent a note to director John Huston asking, "Have you read any good stories lately with a small part in it for a girl who's good at falling off horses?"

Motherhood was Audrey's greatest role, but it would not come easy. Time after time, she could not carry a baby to term. Four times in all. When Audrey was thirty-one, success finally arrived—a son named Sean. A second son, Luca, would follow. Her sons, the two men she would always love the most, brought with them enough smiles to cover the tears.

"Even when I was a little girl, what I wanted most was to have a child. That was the real me. The movies were fairy tales."

"I guess I was just born to be a mother, and if I could have had more than two sons, if I could have had daughters as well, and dozens of them, then I certainly would."

"I had waited my whole life for the moment of giving birth, and it finally happened. I'm sure it's great when you're eighteen, but I was thirty and the long wait made it much sweeter."

"Like all new mothers, I couldn't believe at first he was really for me, and I could really keep him. I'm still filled with wonder of being able to go out and come back—and find he's still there!"

"It is a marvelous thing—a transference—that happens to women when they have children. You become so interested in their lives and their growing. Now, will that look phony in print?"

Be Present

Balancing a career and motherhood is a challenge for any woman, but Audrey found it harder than most. Filming required her to be absent for months at a time in exotic locations with long hours. Once school required that her boys be at home—well, it was just too much.

She decided motherhood must come first. No more long-distance telephone calls and missed bedtime stories. Never again having to say, "When I get home, we will." At the height of her success, Audrey just stayed home.

She walked Luca, her youngest, to school, baked brownies, and did the housework. Her sons were better because of it. Of course, so was she.

"Maybe to my shame I should say I've never taken acting very seriously. The work was important, yes, but not to me. I was very involved in my private life. I came home to a husband, and a child, and marketing."

"I have the greatest admiration for women who can do . . . all three: who have a career, who take care of their husband, and take care of their children. . ."

"The fact that I've made movies doesn't mean breakfast gets made or that my child does better in his homework. I still have to function as a woman in a household."

"I'm functioning as a woman should function and I don't think I'm robbing anybody of anything . . . but by working as a busy film actress I think I would be robbing my family, you know, my husband and children, of the attention they should get."

"First I realized that I had a mom, and she was a pretty great mom. And then I realized she was an actress and she was involved with films. It was only much later that I realized how much she was appreciated worldwide. . . . I think people love her for the right reasons and I think she was deserving of that love."

—her son, Sean Hepburn Ferrer

"She used to surprise my friends with how casual she was. They expected something incredible and instead found just a nice person."

—her son, Luca Dotti

Teach Your Children Well

By tradition, Swiss children begin learning a second national language at the age of eleven. Most end up fluent in at least two. But those would not be the only lessons. There was much more to know.

What She Said

"There's one thing about children that makes them fortunate. Children have only friends. Children have no enemies."

"Never let yourself grow up believing that . . . anybody is any different from anybody else . . . we're all the same."

How to Build Relationships for Life

SIX

Friendship

"The roots of his friendship
Forever profound and powerful;
The firm branches of his affection
Shelter those he loves."

A friend leaves a warm bed on a rainy night to dole out two consecutive boxes of Kleenex. Picks up the phone even though there are only a few minutes to spare. Skips Friday night dinner plans to shake up the ultimate "I hate him" martini. A friend brings ice cream.

Sometimes we qualify them: high school friend, college friend, best friend, family friend, work friend, acquaintance. Yet, no matter how you find them, a friend makes the world a much brighter place.

A true friendship will survive disagreements, new jobs, new relationships, family insanity, and moves across country. It transcends any distance, any timeline, any lifestyle.

True friends are the family we choose.

"[Givenchy's] are the only clothes in which I feel myself. He is far from a couturier, he is a creator of personality."

Be Loyal

Everyone fell in love with Audrey. Her genuine spirit and warm heart attracted all types and her devotion held them close. No one had a bad word to say about her.

Her most famous friendship was with couturier Hubert de Givenchy. She walked into his Paris studio and found not only the clothes wonderful, but also the man.

When Paramount costumer Edith Head got an Oscar for the landmark clothes in *Sabrina*, designs created by Givenchy, Audrey called to apologize. She said she would never let it happen again and she kept her promise.

"She embraced everyone as an acquaintance, but very few people were admitted to her inner circle. She had the ability to keep people at a distance without being in the least bit rough or unkind. Her magnetism was so extraordinary, though, that everyone wanted to be close to her."

—Stanley Donen

"You find out who your real friends are when you're involved in a scandal."

—Elizabeth Taylor

"Wherever she was, in Europe or America, people respected her. I can't think of anybody else that I have worked with that would have such devotion from her friends."

—Bob Willoughby
PHOTOGRAPHER

"Once she sensed that she could trust somebody, she'd do anything for them. And if she were disappointed in them, it would be the end of the world for her."

—Robert Wolders

Love Much

Thoughtfulness was Audrey's hallmark. At the end of *My Fair Lady*, Audrey gave her long-time hairdresser Frank McCoy a Yorkshire Terrier puppy as thanks. His name: Henry Higgins, of course.

When it came to accepting awards or praise, she stood nervously at the podium giving away all the credit. "I really am a product of those men. I'm no Laurence Olivier, no virtuoso talent. I'm basically rather inhibited and I find it difficult to do things in front of people. What my directors have had in common is that they've made me feel so secure, made me feel loved. I depend terribly on them." Now *that's* style.

Never was there an actor, director, designer, photographer, grip, or gaffer who did not fall in love with her. When it came to gratitude, Audrey ranked up there with the all-time experts.

"I think he loved me and I loved him. I think it's rather different. I think it's better than being in love."
—AH on William Wyler

"Audrey definitely had a good heart, there was nothing mean or petty—it's a character thing. She had a good character, so I think people picked up on that too. She didn't have any of the backstabbing, grasping, petty, gossipy personalities that you see in this business. I liked her a lot; in fact, I loved Audrey. It was easy to love her."

—Gregory Peck

"My passion for her has lasted through four marriages—two of hers and two of mine."

—Stanley Donen

"I had the opportunity to see how deep her soul is, and its commitment to life. . . . The love that the woman exuded was absolutely fathomless."

—Harry Belafonte

"She was the best that we could possibly be. She was perfectly charming and perfectly loving. She was a dream; she was the dream that you remember when you wake up smiling."

—Richard Dreyfuss

Listen Well

Italian bombshell Sophia Loren was a close confidante
of Audrey. Imagine two of the world's greatest movie
stars in the kitchen talking
about traveling, husbands,
infertility, and miscarriages,
usually over pasta.

> "I like to talk to very close friends
> about feelings, but I hate chatter."

While Audrey rarely sought out advice, she would
dispense it willingly. Often her sensible, heartfelt
approach was just what one needed to hear. Audrey
knew that nothing felt better than a good gab with a
good friend. Pasta or not.

What They Said

"Audrey really cared and really listened. Most people don't. If you
really listen, it's because you really care. I don't listen to half of
what I hear—but Audrey did."

—Doris Brynner

"She had that rare capacity to listen to people and come up with
the right advice, by instinct as much as anything."

—Christa Roth
UNICEF executive

Givenchy on Audrey

When Audrey first met Hubert de Givenchy, she was hardly a household name in France, as the film *Roman Holiday* had not yet been released there. Givenchy was told that Miss Hepburn was coming to look for clothes for her new movie *Sabrina*, and naturally thought only of Katharine.

"But when the door of my studio opened, there stood a young woman, very slim, very tall, with doe eyes and short hair and wearing a pair of narrow pants, a little T shirt, slippers and a gondolier's hat with red ribbon that read *Venezia*. I told her, 'Mademoiselle, I would love to help you, but I have very few sewers, I am in the middle of doing a collection, I can't make you clothes.' So she said, 'Show me what you have already made for the collection.' She tried on

> **"I depend on Givenchy in the same way that American women depend on their psychiatrists. There are few people I love more. He is the single person I know with the greatest integrity."**

the dresses—'It's exactly what I need!'—and they fit her too."

They went to dinner that night. "It was then that she truly won my heart. She told me of her life, her passion for the dance, her discovery by Colette. I saw that she was a woman very different from the others, and I felt an extraordinary sympathy with her."

"Audrey, who was always of admirable fidelity and loyalty, never forgot that first meeting. She had been very touched that I had consented to help her, even though I didn't know her. For each of the films that she made afterwards, she wanted me to dress her or help in the fittings of costumes that were not in my usual sphere."

Their collaboration would not only turn out a stunning new style, aptly named *décolleté Sabrina*, but also a deep friendship that only grew stronger as the years went on.

Laugh Often

Laughing *at* is mean, but laughing *with* is magic. Especially when it was with Audrey.

Audrey knew that laughter was the fastest way to friendship. Her sense of humor, while rarely shared with the public, brought her friends close. Just when things seemed at their worst, she always managed to crack a joke to keep everyone smiling.

"I love people who make me laugh. I honestly think it's the thing I like most, to laugh. It cures a multitude of ills. It's probably the most important thing in a person."

"Most people think of Audrey Hepburn as regal. I like to think of her as spunky. . . . She was a cutup, she was a clown. I think that would surprise people who didn't know her. She could always make me laugh between scenes . . . she was a comic."

—Gregory Peck

"We had big jokes, and she was funny. She was always looking with wide eyes at the happenings in Hollywood. She just did not know—she thought that she was a beginner, that she was just starting to act."

—Billy Wilder

"Her secret was her bubble—an internal bubble that you were waiting to come out—of humor."

—Roger Moore

"I used to always think that I'd look back on us crying and laugh, but, I never thought I'd look back on us laughing and cry."

—Ralph Waldo Emerson

Be Genuine

Audrey littered her tables and bookshelves with memories of movie sets, first steps, and exotic movie locations. The only photo she kept of herself was a signed Cecil Beaton portrait. And even that was tucked away behind the rest.

For all the grand, gala occasions she attended, it was the simple pleasures of togetherness—usually in the kitchen—that would mean the most.

What They Said

"Audrey and I decided we'd throw a party for the cast and the crew when the picture was finished. We went all out, had it catered by Romanoff's—nothing but the best. In the middle of the party, Audrey sidled up to me, jabbed me with her elbow and said, out of the corner of her mouth, 'Hey, Shirl-Girl, whattya think the bruise is gonna be for this bash?'"

—Shirley MacLaine

"Audrey sensed very early in her life and career that
self-worth based on fame or beauty is very short-lived,
and so she remained forever herself—realistic, aware,
and caring."

—her husband, Robert Wolders

How to Make the Most of It

seven
Fulfillment

"We are all grown-up children,
really. Our lives are made up of
adulthood and childhood, all
together. So one should go back in
search of what was loved and
found to be real."

The Rolling Stones couldn't get it. Hamlet had to die for it. Henry David Thoreau wandered in the woods to find it. Sinatra found it his way.

Satisfaction.

We are more lonely, more overworked and more stressed out than ever before. We have somehow forgotten about what really matters. If only we could find a few more moments: leaving the office early to make a child's soccer game; perfecting a soufflé; a phone call to an old friend; a handwritten thank-you note.

Before electricity, satisfaction was found in purpose, serenity, laughter, joy, companionship, growth, and spirituality. Through all this progress, maybe we haven't changed that much after all.

Distinguish Between Lonely and Alone

By nature, Audrey was reserved and shy. As a child, making friends was not always easy. Add to that an absent father, a less than tolerant mother and a war.

While Audrey may have preferred to share her time with others, instead she read books, took long walks, listened to music, and arranged flowers. She found solitude in the stillness. In Hollywood, Audrey was sometimes called aloof. Instead of parties and dinners out, she spent most of her time at home.

She would be the last to say so, but deep down Audrey knew she could survive anything that life threw her way. She knew that she could handle it—alone.

"I have to be alone quite often. I'd be quite happy if I spent Saturday night to Monday morning in my apartment. That's how I refuel."

"I had very little real youth, few friends, little fun in the usual teenage way, and no security. Is it any wonder I became an interior sort of person?"

"I'm an introvert . . . I love being by myself, love being outdoors, love taking a long walk with my dogs and looking at trees, flowers, the sky."

"It can be very lonely in a crowd."

"Being alone, I recharge my batteries."

"When the chips are down, you are alone, and loneliness can be terrifying. Fortunately, I've always had a chum I could call. And I love to be alone. It doesn't bother me one bit. I'm my own company."

Behind the Scenes

WAR AND PEACE

"I did *War and Peace* in
velvets and furs in August. . . .
In the hunting scene where I'm in velvet and
a high hat, the family was plodding across a big
field in the blazing Roman sunshine and, all of a
sudden, my horse fainted out from under me. They
quickly got me out of the saddle . . . So when they say
I'm strong as a horse, I am. I'm stronger! I didn't faint. The
horse did."

Get a Therapist

While Audrey found enough therapy digging around in the garden, she knew that some of us need a bit more help.

Her marriage to Italian psychiatrist Andrea Dotti gave her a firsthand look at what therapy had to offer. Fascinated with his "constant struggle to fight against suffering," Audrey learned a lot.

Audrey knew that understanding ends in compassion. And if a little therapy would do the trick, well then, just get on with it.

"There are people who blow their tops, and people who don't. I am told it is bad to bottle it all up inside you, but then if you blow you have to go around apologizing . . .
I suppose I should just let it come out of my ears."

"We are all involved in psychiatry, whether we know it or not; the processes are all so applicable to living. Why should it be frightening to live with a psychiatrist? He is just someone who understands people a little bit more than anyone else. And that's great. Then, there is more understanding in general and a more compassionate relationship to live with—more patience."

"It is important to know as much as possible about the workings of someone you love, no? It should help your life, not frighten. No one should be scared to go to the doctor. I think it is very admirable to try to get over one's problems yourself, but when and if it becomes agonizing, people should try to get help. I mean, one can treat a cold, but if you develop a raging fever, you call a doctor."

Audrey's Book Club

As a child, Audrey devoured books. Among her favorites were Rudyard Kipling's *The Jungle Book*, Joanna Spyri's *Heidi*, and Frances Hodgson Burnett's *The Secret Garden*.

Throughout her life, reading would remain an important pastime. She was an adult when she received *The Diary of Anne Frank* in the mail. From her view out an attic window, Anne wrote of the ravages of World War II, and of a spirit transformed by human suffering. Both Anne and Audrey were ten when the war began. It nearly destroyed her.

"It was in a different corner of Holland, [but] all the events I experienced were so incredibly accurately described by her—not just what was going on on the outside, but what was going on on the inside of a young girl starting to be a woman . . . all in a cage. She expresses the claustrophobia, but transcends it through her love of nature, her awareness of humanity and her love—real love—of life.

"People all have fears, but mostly they are distant and unknown to them. They are afraid of death which they haven't gone through, they are afraid of getting cancer which they don't have, they are afraid of getting run over which hasn't happened. But I've known the cold clutch of human terror. I've seen it, I've felt it, I've heard it."

"This was my life. I didn't know what I was going to read. I've never been the same again, it affected me so deeply."

Practice Acceptance

Audrey often spoke about her insecurities, perhaps the worst of which focused on her looks. But her friend and neighbor Doris Brynner would never believe her.

"Audrey was a mass of complexes—she thought she was too flat-chested, she thought her feet were too big. We used to get together, and if she was in that kind of mood, she'd say, 'Why can't I have small feet like you?' Which was ridiculous, because she was perfect-looking!"

One day, Audrey appeared on her doorstep with no makeup, held up her face and said, "See how square it is?" To us, she was perfect. And eventually she started to believe us. But to Doris, she would always be just "Square."

"When you're young, I suppose it's natural to pick someone you want to look like. I wanted to be a cross between Elizabeth Taylor and Ingrid Bergman. I didn't do either, either."

"I'm the sort of person who has done the best with what I've had. I was too thin and I had no bosom to speak of. Add them up, and a girl can feel terribly self-conscious."

"I would have no sooner thought of my face on the screen as I would that anyone would want me for anything at all in the movie line. I didn't think much of my looks. In fact, I thought I was such an ugly thing that no one would ever want me for a wife."

"I must have an odd face, they can make it up to look wise. I am not."

"The greatest victory in my life has been to be able to live with myself, to accept my shortcomings and those of others. I'm a long way from being the human being I'd like to be. But I've decided I'm not so bad after all."

FUNNY FACE

"Oh no! You could
never make a
model out of
that. I think my
face is perfectly
funny!"

—Jo Stockton

Find a Peaceful Place

Switzerland held a special place in Audrey's heart. A neutral country, Audrey felt protected from war, just as her mother once had in their Dutch homeland.

But it was La Paisable, an eighteenth-century stone farmhouse with eight bedrooms and its white picket fence, that kept her there for good. With less than five hundred year-round residents, Audrey shared daily life only with loved ones, the farmers, and the occasional cow. It was close enough to the city, but surrounded by the peaks of the Swiss Alps, vineyards, fruit orchards, and the shores of Lake Geneva.

For Audrey, home was "worth more than a second Oscar." And what a home it was.

"I was here when I had the first glance of the house and it was spring and fruit trees were in blossom, and my heart stopped beating. I said, 'This is my place!'"

"It's everything I long for. All my life, what I wanted to earn money for was to have a house of my own. I dreamed of having a house in the country with a garden and fruit trees. I've lived in Switzerland for more than half my life. I love it. I love the country. I love our little town. The shops. I love going to the open market twice a week with all the fruit and vegetables and flowers."

"As you get older, it's nice to feel you belong somewhere—having lived a rather circus life."

"[Switzerland] is the absolute opposite of the life I led working. I was to a great extent left in peace. The Swiss press doesn't care what you do."

"There is no place in the world where I feel so much at peace. It's my private stomping ground. I've become one of these people. We're loyal to each other."

"She really wasn't the Hollywood type. She worked there—rented a house, did the job—and then came back to Switzerland. . . . We were always pushing her to make another movie, but the only thing she really looked forward to was staying home."

—Doris Brynner,
CLOSE FRIEND

"She loved just being home with her family. We'd have dinner in the kitchen and she loved sour apples for dessert. She certainly respected and loved her career, but her family came first . . ."

—Connie Wald,
CLOSE FRIEND

Live Simply

At home, Audrey focused on one thing at a time—
shopping, cooking, reading, gardening. This was the
stuff of life. The stuff that really mattered, anyway.

Robert Wolders, a man with the same sensibility
and her greatest companion, explained: "Some of our
friends regarded us as antisocial. Days at home would
be very leisurely—a stroll in the afternoon, in the vineyards with the dogs. A swim, if the weather allowed it
and then, at night, a friend or two. And
that's what gave her the most pleasure."

For Audrey, life was in the details.

"Living is like tearing
through a museum.
Not until later do you
really start absorbing
what you saw, thinking
about it, looking it up
in a book and
remembering—
because you can't
take it all in at once."

"It is because I live in the country in Switzerland that I can lead a totally unselfconscious life and be totally myself. I have a delightful rose garden and I have an orchard and jams and jellies to preserve."

"It's going to sound like a thumping bore, but my idea of heaven is [having] Robert and my two sons at home—I hate separations—and the dogs, a good movie, a wonderful meal, and great television all coming together. I'm really blissful when that happens. [My goal] was not to have huge luxuries. As a child, I wanted a house with a garden, which I have today. That is what I dreamed of."

"I adore cooking and love to garden. Dull, isn't it?"

"I want to be home with my family. Now, how does that look in print? But I really do. I am quite a simple person."

"She took an immense delight in having a quiet dinner with friends and saying, 'Oh, it's still light, let's go for a walk'—a walk which was way off the roads, down the cow tracks, up and down, over and across everything, very swift. Not exactly a leisurely stroll. She liked to move, very much appreciating each environment she came to . . . and she got you to appreciate it as well."

—Michael Tilson Thomas
COMPOSER

137

Have Faith

Raised as a Christian Scientist, like her mother, Audrey found faith in humanity, in the goodness of people, in the miracle of nature to be re-born year after year. Most of all, her faith was strongest in her love— the ability to give all of oneself and make a difference.

Maybe that's why her gardens were always so full of flowers.

"[I have] enormous faith, but it's not attached to any one particular religion . . . My mother was one thing, my father another. In Holland they were all Calvinists. That has no importance at all to me."

"Anyone who does not believe in miracles is not a realist."

"I am no longer a Christian Scientist, but I believe in something—in the strength, maybe, of the human spirit."

"My only religion is a belief in nature."

"Faith is the bird that feels the light and sings when the dawn is still dark."

—Rabindranath Tagore

Be Needed

Audrey loved to be loved, just like the rest of us. Never was it about receiving, but so much more. As a wife and mother, she was devoted and attentive. As a friend, she was loyal and kind. As a star, she was all of the above.

Her mother always impressed on her the idea of generosity. Audrey's heart was the greatest gift she had to give.

"My mother always impressed upon us, you have to be useful, to be needed and to be able to give love. I think it's even more important than receiving it."

"I was born with an enormous need for affection. I have always been terribly aware of it, even when I was small. And a terrible need to give it, like every child—they all want a dog, they want a cat, they all want a horse, they all want to cuddle a baby. That has been very strong with me."

"When you have nobody you can make a cup of tea for, when nobody needs you, that's when I think life is over."

"When you can't contribute anymore, that's when you start feeling old and you feel as though it's the beginning of the end. . . . Loneliness, not solitude, because I like solitude, but that's the kind of loneliness which is sad about aging, if that happens."

"[So] It isn't age or even death that one fears, as much as loneliness and the lack of affection . . . Why are people so anguished? Always it's a balance of affection that people have had in life, the loneliness, and what they have missed."

How to Be an Icon

eight

Style

"I never think of myself as an icon.
What is in other people's minds is
not in my mind. I just do my thing."

ing Louis XIV was the first to see that fashion is a mirror (in velvet and lace, mind you). Clothes have a language all their own. They tell our age, gender, wealth, and profession. The choices we make are quite revealing.

Fashion is a creative reflection of our cultural times. Influenced by musicians, politicians, celebrities, and other cultural royalty, it is for public consumption. Style, on the other hand, is a more private matter. Style comes from somewhere on the inside.

Know Yourself

In *Funny Face*, the ultimate fashion musical, Audrey's role tapped into more of her personality than you might think. Just like Audrey, Jo Stockton was wise, defiant, romantic, good-hearted, and stunning. Of course, she was also hypercritical.

Audrey's insecurities led to a certain type of precision. Early on, Audrey decided what looked good on and what did not.

Her choices were always right. Who can forget Sabrina's falling-in-love gown or Holly's oh-so-glamorous little black dress? Her fashion impact resonates to this day. But then again, excellence never does go out of style.

"I think any woman dresses mostly for the man in her life."

"I have worked from twelve and I know my body well. I am not a beauty. Taken one by one, my features are not really good. When I work, I rely on my studio hairdresser and make-up man."

"You have to look at yourself objectively. Analyze yourself like an instrument. You have to be absolutely frank with yourself. Face your handicaps, don't try to hide them. Instead, develop something else."

"Some people dream of having a big swimming pool— with me, it's closets."

"It seems to me that it is within the reach of every woman to develop a similar individuality of style by learning to know herself."

"Her personal style was a result of her unwillingness to compromise on these values and to focus on what is basic and real. She showed a great deal of stubbornness to outside influences, always insisting on what felt natural and comfortable. Her sense of appropriateness and decorum was happily mixed with a sense of irony and humor—not taking herself too seriously, but seriously enough."

—Robert Wolders

SABRINA

"She knew exactly how to shape her strong, independent image. This naturally extended to the way she dressed. And she always took the clothes created for her one step further by adding something of her own, some small personal detail which enhanced the whole. But it wasn't only elegance that she enhanced. She heightened the impact of the entire design."

—Hubert de Givenchy

ℒess ℐs ℳore

Audrey was haute to couture. Her style, and its evolution, simultaneously defies and defines fashion. Even opera diva Maria Callas modeled herself after her.

Audrey clothes were the product of a certain mutual philosophy. Originated by Balenciaga, well-executed by Givenchy, and strongly influenced by Audrey.

Hers was a closet built on quality, not quantity. The pieces were deceptively simple—a black dress, a white wrap blouse, a tasteful suit. Not always the latest, simply the best.

"I have no time to shop for 'Audrey' clothes. I have two dinner dresses and slacks, and horrible gaps in between."

"Balenciaga once said the secret of elegance is elimination. I believe that. That's why I love Hubert Givenchy . . . They're clothes without ornament, with everything stripped away."

"You take the frills away, the bows away, the 'this' away, you really see the line of something."

"You can wear Hubert's clothes until they are worn out and still be elegant."

"She always underdressed instead of overdressed. Nobody in the world looked better in plain white pants and a white blouse. Whatever she put on became perfectly elegant. Without a stick of jewelry, she looked like a queen."

—Eva Gabor

"[Audrey] rarely skimped on quality. If she wore a shirt, it was a good shirt, a first class shirt! Or a first class hat! . . . But simple—I mean, if she was gardening, or cooking, or something like that."

—Audrey Wilder
CLOSE FRIEND

FUNNY FACE

"Audrey and I agreed she would wear black tight-fitting pants, a black sweater and black shoes. I wanted her to wear white socks with it, and she was stunned. 'Absolutely not!' she said. 'It will spoil the whole black silhouette and cut the line at my feet!' I said, 'If you don't wear the white socks you will fade into the background . . .' She burst into tears and ran into her dressing room. After a little while she regained her composure, put on the white socks, returned to the set and went ahead without a whimper.

"Later, when she saw the sequence, she sent me a note saying, 'You were right about the socks. Love, Audrey.'"

—Stanley Donen

Comfort Is Crucial

Being comfortable counted as much toward style as anything else (note Audrey's ballerina flats). Very little make-up and even less jewelry and *voilà*! A men's white button-down never looked so good.

But finding clothes beyond Givenchy was not always easy. Eventually, she would turn to Ralph Lauren for his European sense of American style. At home, she needed T-shirts and sweaters and, yes, even jeans.

"Shirts are so wonderful. All you do is wash and iron them."

"I've got this figure of mine that looks impossible in off-the-rack clothes. If the length's right, then the top swims on me. It's very discouraging to see yourself looking practically malformed. I loathe trying on clothes."

"Who can afford to dress all the time at Givenchy's? I can't. Really. I get one or two suits from him. Dresses for grand, gala occasions. But all the time? Oh no."

"First of all, even if you had the money you wouldn't want to buy them. You spend now on one evening dress what it would have cost to buy full wardrobes for two years."

"I'm always in sweaters and pants. I have very few good clothes. I have to take care of them. I take them off as soon as I get upstairs."

"You could take Audrey into Sears Roebuck or Givenchy or Ralph Lauren or an army surplus store—it didn't matter, she'd put something on and you'd say, 'It's her!' . . . Clothes look great or not depending on who's wearing them."

—Ralph Lauren

Avoid Trends

In public, Audrey was an arbiter of taste and style. Her friends, Hubert de Givenchy and Ralph Lauren, enveloped her with just the right fabric and drape. In the late sixties, she even managed to make Pucci-like color look elegant.

Only once, when Audrey left Hollywood for a life less glamorous as a Roman housewife, did she falter. Out of the spotlight, her style edged a bit too close to dowdy. Still, it was the seventies; nobody escaped unharmed. Soon enough her fashion sense returned to peak form.

"I love clothes to where it is practically a vice."

"Why change? Everyone has his own style. When you have found it, you should stick to it."

"I want to stay in fashion. But being young in spirit counts more toward looking young than dressing in a hippy style."

"I've never even thought of myself as very glamorous: Glamorous is Ava Gardner or Elizabeth Taylor, not me."

"My look is attainable. Women can look like Audrey Hepburn by flipping out their hair, buying the large sunglasses, and the little sleeveless dresses."

"I just hope I didn't upset too many mothers if their daughters cut off their hair or whatever to copy me."

"She said, 'I can't decide if I should wear the pantsuit or the dress. Let me model them for you.' . . . She disappeared and came back wearing this stunning understated Givenchy creation which hugged her gorgeous frame. I was absolutely dumbstruck. After a moment, she looked at me very kindly and said, "I guess you prefer the dress."

—Michael Tilson Thomas

ROMAN HOLIDAY

PRINCESS ANN: I hate this nightgown. I hate all my nightgowns, and I hate all my underwear too.

COUNTESS: My dear, you have lovely things.

PRINCESS ANN: But I'm not two hundred years old. Why can't I sleep in pajamas?

COUNTESS: Pajamas!?

PRINCESS ANN: Just the top part. Did you know that there are people who sleep with absolutely nothing on at all?

COUNTESS: I rejoice to say I do not.

Style for Life

Despite a torrid love affair with white country roses, Audrey's Swiss home was filled with color. The butter-white walls of the living room boasted bold botanicals. Bright yellow couches and an all-white seating area begged for good conversation. Fresh flowers mixed in with charming duck decoys for that extra special touch. And tucked away in a small back foyer, her beloved canaries gave shelter to her very own white porcelain pig.

Simply lavish, classically comfortable, fun and fantastic—Audrey's home was an expression of what she valued most.

"It's the flowers you choose, the music you play, the smile you have waiting. I want it to be gay and cheerful, a haven in this troubled world."

"A house isn't a home if a child and a dog can't go into the main room."

"I cannot look back with nostalgia at a coat I enjoyed wearing years ago. I was inside it, and it kept me warm, but I am still here and the coat is something of the past."

"What I always wanted, what I still want, is to create a warm and loving atmosphere for those I care about—my family and friends."

"Most apartments in Rome are so heavy, with those heavy drapes and heavy, ornate paintings, and gold. But Audrey's was totally different—bright and airy, lovely yellow and white. Her draperies were the kind of material that would lie on the floor. They actually draped. All those other apartments looked like lasagna by comparison."

—Audrey Wilder

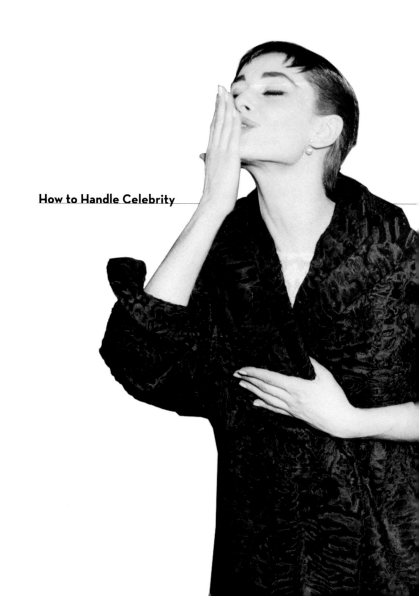

How to Handle Celebrity

Fame

"Not only was there never a moment when I thought, 'Oh, now I'm going to be a star,' but I promise you, even now I never feel I've become all that."

owadays anyone can get those fifteen minutes that Andy Warhol predicted—slick lawyers, wealthy computer geeks, randy politicians, scandalous madams, naïve adulteresses, suburban murderers, brave bug-eaters, and glitzy heiresses. Talent is no longer a requirement.

In public, celebrities do their jobs: attend movie premieres, sign autographs, dress up in haute couture, perform concerts. When the work is done, they buy groceries, walk their dogs, visit with friends, and take their kids to the park. They are just human, like everybody else.

Some say stalking paparazzi, tabloid rumors, and interrupted lunches are worth the price. But fame is an illusion. It won't fix anything.

It is the inside that counts.

"Please don't say I'm self-effacing. You have to face something to be self-effacing."

Never Be Too Sure

Her American career shows only nineteen films in forty-two years. The roles that first come to mind are *Roman Holiday*, *Sabrina*, *Breakfast at Tiffany's* and *My Fair Lady*. The more diverse choices, where Audrey tested her talent, are often less noted: *The Nun's Story*, *Two for the Road*, and *Wait Until Dark*.

To the world, Audrey would forever be a princess in a fairytale. In her own life, she felt much the same.

What She Said

"Truly, I've never been concerned with any public image. It would drive me around the bend if I worried about the pedestal others have put me on. And also I don't believe it."

"I don't have an image of myself at all. It's in the public's eye."

"It's not that I've got more valuable, it's inflation that's got higher."

When Necessary, Talk Back

The rumors began when they starred together in *War and Peace* as newlyweds: Mel Ferrer was influencing Audrey to choose only projects that benefited his career. Even her mother had her suspicions.

Certainly Mel struck some shrewd deals on their behalf. One deal lent her to Paramount to make *Funny Face* in return for an MGM movie where Audrey would star and Mel would direct. The result was *Green Mansions*, a box office flop.

Defending Mel was the first time Audrey had to handle the darkest side of celebrity. Though Audrey did some of her best work when she was also Mrs. Ferrer, she eventually saw more truth in the rumor than she initially thought. Still, you can't blame a girl for trying.

PHIL DONAHUE: You never became an egomaniac?

AUDREY: How do you know?

"How can people say Mel makes all my decisions, that he decides what I am going to play, and with whom, and where! It so infuriates me. I know how scrupulously correct he is, and how he loathes to give an opinion unless I ask for it."

"After it was decided, Mel and I were thrilled at the thought of being in the same picture together. But from that moment on, we were put on the defensive. Imagine! Two married people, in the same profession, whose interests and careers are parallel, having to give excuses for playing in the same film together!"

"Surely it's a natural reaction for him to steer me through the crowds and look after me? It's the natural reaction of a man, and my husband is a man and not a Svengali."

"If you lead a simple life, and that story is written, then that story will not satisfy. It needs an angle. Suppose there is no angle?"

"I don't care what is written about me so long as it is true."

—Katharine Hepburn

BREAKFAST AT TIFFANY'S

"'Moon River' was written for Audrey. No one else has ever understood it so completely. There have been more than a thousand versions of 'Moon River,' but hers is unquestionably the definitive one."

—Henry Mancini

Have a Purpose

At the height of her celebrity, Audrey left movies behind to find what she knew to be real—home and family.

While she was away, movies began to take a new turn. Television delivered the world's worst tragedies into our living rooms. Entertainment and news were forever altered—violence was in.

Audrey had loved her movies all along, yet suddenly she saw their purpose more clearly.

"The world has always been cynical, and I think I'm a romantic at heart. I hope for better things, and I thank God the world is also full of people who want to be genuine and kind."

"I am proud to have been in a business that gives pleasure, creates beauty, and awakens our conscience, arouses compassion, and pehaps most importantly, gives millions a respite from our so violent world."

"If I ever want to accentuate the importance of anything in any form of entertainment, it is the quality of the fairy tale. . . . People go to the theater and the cinema for the same reason that makes them like fairy tales—the sense of watching something that isn't real. The fairy tale is, to my mind, the core of entertainment."

"People associate me with a time when movies were pleasant, when women wore pretty dresses in films and you heard beautiful music. I always love it when people write to me and say, 'I was having a rotten time, and I walked into a cinema and saw one of your movies, and it made such a difference.'"

Give Back

Audrey spent her career creating art and her fame creating humanity.

We adored the tender vulnerability she shared on screen. She adored her life at home as a devoted mother, committed wife and loving friend. At fifty-nine, Audrey had all she had ever hoped for and much more than she could ever have imagined.

Still, she decided there was more to be done. As a goodwill ambassador for UNICEF, she traveled the world, rallying politicians, relief workers and all of humankind to care for the world's neediest children. Without a doubt, it was her greatest achievement of all.

"It's not a sacrifice. Because a sacrifice means you give up something you want for something you don't want. This is no sacrifice, it's a gift I am receiving."

What She Said

"Whatever baggage you're given—fame if you like—creates curiosity. People want to see you. I'm using the curiosity for the children."

Humanity

How to Change the World

"It's ironic that it was because of children that I stayed home all these years. Now it is for the sake of the children that I'm traveling all over the world."

Most of us accept that when we flip the light switch, the bulb will light up the darkness. When we turn on the tap, crystalline water will pour deliciously into our glass. When we are hungry, there will be something to eat. We also accept that others do not deserve the same.

In the cities, we walk by the homeless each and every day. On the nightly news, we glorify hatred and rage. In entertainment, we celebrate the discomfort of others. We have learned to accept the unacceptable. It is a tragedy.

Changing the world seems an impossible task. And not one among us can do it. Only when we each commit to small steps forward will we turn it all around.

Think Deeply

UNICEF, the United Nations Children's Fund, relies entirely on voluntary contributions to perform much-needed relief work around the world.

Audrey's role as a goodwill ambassador was to travel to the countries that were in the greatest need, witness the problems firsthand, meet the people, watch the progress, and report back to the rest of the world. She would increase awareness and raise funds.

In her years of service, the U.S. Committee for UNICEF nearly doubled its fund-raising revenue. In 1992, she received the United States' highest civilian honor, the Presidential Medal of Freedom. Audrey came to UNICEF with two main qualifications: a big name and a big heart. But it was what she learned that made the difference.

"Mothers are the best social workers of all."

"The question I am most frequently asked is 'What do you really do for UNICEF?' To fully understand the problems of the world's children, it would be nice to be an expert on education, economics, politics, religions, traditions, and cultures. I am none of these things, but I am a mother."

"You can't just get up and say, 'Oh, I'm happy to be here, and I love children.' No, that's not enough. It's not even enough to know there has been a flood in Bangladesh and seven thousand people lost their lives. Why the flood? What is their history? Why are they one of the poorest countries of today? How are they going to survive? Are they getting enough help? What are the statistics? What are their problems?"

"Somebody said to me the other day, 'You know, it's really senseless, what you're doing. There's always been suffering, there will always be suffering, and you're just prolonging the suffering of these children [by rescuing them].' My answer is, 'Okay, then, let's start with your grandchild. Don't buy antibiotics if it gets pneumonia. Don't take it to the hospital if it has an accident.' It's against life—against humanity—to think that way."

Don't Get Political

As a goodwill ambassador for UNICEF, one cannot take political stands. It is an international organization that works for the good of all countries, regardless of race, religion, or politics. With rare exception, Audrey followed the rules and instead did what she did best: brought out the humanity in us all.

However, in 1992, when asked to identify the biggest obstacle UNICEF faced, she replied simply, "War. The developing countries spend about $150 billion on arms each year. Meanwhile, the five permanent members of the UN Security Council sell ninety percent of the world's arms."

"The minute something happens to a child, you pick it up and take it to the hospital. You don't think about religion or politics."

"UNICEF's mandate is to protect every child against famine, thirst, sickness, abuse, and death, but today we are dealing with a far more ominous threat—the dark side of humanity: the selfishness, avarice, aggression which have already polluted our skies, emptied our oceans, destroyed our forests and extinguished thousands of beautiful animals. Are our children next?"

"How is it that governments spend so much on warfare and bypass the needs of their children, their greatest capital, their only hope for peace?"

"Each country has huge problems of its own, which quite rightly they must take care of—the homeless in America, the poor in every country. But I think there's always enough to give to the countries that are the most needy."

"Survival means much, much more than a Band-Aid. I wouldn't call a good doctor that saves your child from dying a Band-Aid. You may say that only tiny numbers of people can be helped. But the numbers are getting bigger. I go through my soul-searching. What can I do? What am I going to go and do there? But for all of us there's something we can do. It's true you can't take care of a thousand. But, finally, if you can save one, I'd be glad to do that."

Be Hands-on

In the copilot's seat, Audrey sat silent, awed by the stark quality of the Ethiopian landscape. The year was 1988.

Ethiopia had a long history of famine, drought, and civil war. Believed to be the poorest country in the world, one in four children died by the age of five. In overcrowded refugee camps, the few who survived remained malnourished and many were blind due to a vitamin A deficiency. Civil war staved off the delivery of food sitting in the northern ports.

"The human obligation is to help children who are suffering anywhere in the world. All the rest is luxury and trivial."

In a refugee camp, Audrey saw a little girl standing alone. She went to her and asked her what she wanted to be when she grew up. The girl said simply, "Alive."

"I went into rebel country and saw mothers and their children who had walked for ten days, even three weeks, looking for food, settling onto the desert floor into makeshift camps where they may die. Horrible. That image is too much for me. The 'Third World' is a term I don't like very much, because we're all one world."

"I went with so many people telling me how harrowing and dreadful it would be to see the extent of the suffering, the death, and the despair. But I also witnessed how much is being done to help and how just a small amount of aid can assist in treating the sick, irrigating the land, and planting new crops. I came to realize that Ethiopia's problems are not unsolvable if only the world would give a little more."

"Given a spade, they will dig a well. I do not want to see them digging graves for their children. As Gandhi said, 'Wars cannot be won by bullets but only by bleeding hearts.' I think we can help all these beautiful, silent children."

BANGLADESH

"She smiled at the children, and some of them came forward to stroke her arm and hold her hands . . . just ahead, a small girl sat by herself under the shade of a coconut tree. The little one caught Audrey's attention, and she asked, 'Why doesn't she join the others?' Walking over, Audrey knelt down and spoke with her. Then, picking her up, she hugged her close. The child's legs, crippled by polio, dangled uselessly. Carrying the little one, Audrey walked towards us, her eyes filled with tears. None of the rest of us had taken notice of that child."

—Cole Dodge,
UNICEF REPRESENTATIVE

Nothing Will Prepare You

By the end of 1990, Audrey would complete six additional goodwill missions for UNICEF: Turkey, South America (Venezuela and Ecuador), Central America (Guatemala, Honduras, and El Salvador), the Sudan, Bangladesh, and Vietnam.

In Somalia, ravaged by years of war, famine, and neglect, eight million people were starving to death. At the onset of the rainy season, death tolls were on the rise. While food distribution was improving, without the proper blankets and clothing, the cold night air was often too much. The illiteracy rate was the highest in the world—95 percent.

While she had wanted to go a year earlier, in September 1992 Audrey would take her final mission, and her hardest, to visit the people of Somalia.

"I went through a war. Surely that made me a little more aware that some people might not know what it means to be hungry, deprivation and so forth. Never do I think of that when I see a child in Africa who is at death's door."

"I have seen famine in Ethiopia and Bangladesh, but I have seen nothing like this—so much worse than I could possibly have imagined."

"I want to be very careful how I say this. I don't want to sound overly dramatic. But you really wonder whether God hasn't forgotten Somalia."

"The earth is an extraordinary sight, a deep terra-cotta red. And you see the villages, displacement camps and compounds, and the earth is all rippled around them like an ocean bed; I was told those were the graves. There are graves everywhere. Wherever there is a road, around the paths you take, along the riverbeds, near every camp, there are graves. People who can still walk are phantoms."

"No media report could have prepared me for the unspeakable agony I felt seeing countless little, fragile, emaciated children sitting under the trees, waiting to be fed, most of them ill. I'll never forget their huge eyes and tiny faces and the terrible silence."

"The silence is something you never forget."

Inspire

Audrey set a good example. She taught us many things.

Think of all that she—one woman—accomplished. And imagine the possibilities.

"Since the world has existed, there has been injustice. But it is one world, the more so as it becomes smaller, more accessible. There is just no question that there is a moral obligation that those who have should give to those who have nothing."

"Children are our most vital resource, our hope for the future. Until they can be assured of not only physically surviving the first fragile years of life, but are free of emotional, social, and physical abuse, it is impossible to envisage a world that is free of tension and violence. But it is up to us to make it possible."

"I am filled with a rage at ourselves. I don't believe in collective guilt, but I do believe in collective responsibility."

CONTINUE THE LEGACY

While I have long been a fan of Audrey, it was not until I began researching her work for UNICEF, the United Nations Children's Fund, that I could begin to understand the challenges that they face and the solutions that they create each and every day.

With a hopeful voice, Audrey said, "Is there a solution? We have to believe that, in time, there will be. I go though a lot of soul-searching. I keep sane by saying it is not my job to solve all problems. My job is to help UNICEF save children. And finally, that is the most important thing. Because it is these children who will, we hope, grow up to be healthy, productive citizens. And change their country."

Changing this world is truly up to us—one country, one volunteer and one child at a time. To learn more about UNICEF and how you can make a difference, in the United States write to:

Audrey Hepburn Memorial Fund
c/o U.S. Committe for UNICEF
333 East 38th Street
New York, NY 10016

212-922-2549 or 1-800-FOR-KIDS
http://www.unicef.org

ACKNOWLEDGMENTS

I am forever indebted to Audrey Hepburn for a life well-lived, but also to her family who continue to share her so elegantly with the rest of the world. If you have not already, please read *Audrey Hepburn, An Elegant Spirit: A Son Remembers* by Sean Hepburn Ferrer and support The Audrey Hepburn Children's Fund with your purchase. Please note that this book is in no way authorized by her estate, and they reserve all rights to publish a book of their own in the future.

None of this would be possible without the illustrious list of biographers, interviewers, photographers, and documentarians who captured Audrey throughout the years. In particular: biographer Barry Paris, documentarian Professor Richard Brown, and journalist Barbara Walters.

At the wonderful Dutton Books: Amy Hughes, who saw potential I didn't even show her. Anna Cowles, whose enthusiasm, diligence, and patience honed that potential into reality. And Brian Tart, who took a shot on an unknown, but never let me feel like one.

I am forever indebted to Chris Calhoun, an extraordinary agent and a man so swell that he is sure to go down in the record books. Bill Zehme, my greatest cheerleader and wisest friend. John Davies, who never stopped asking, "Have you done it yet?" Jim Agnew, the king of research. And all my family and friends who lived with me while all this was going on, and loved me anyway. Especially Suzy.

This book is also for Adam—the best man I ever married and the only one I'll ever need. You make my soul fly. Thank you.

SOURCES

Articles

Abramson, Martin. "Audrey Hepburn," *Cosmopolitan*, October 1955, p. 26-32.

"Audrey Hepburn—Angel of Love," undated Dutch article, translated by Sandra Homner.

"Audrey Hepburn," *Movie & T.V. Album*, July 1957.

"Audrey Hepburn's Fashion Formula," *Los Angeles Times Magazine*, November 11, 1962.

"Audrey Hepburn: Many Sided Charmer," *Life* magazine, December 7, 1953.

"Audrey Stars in Givenchy Styles," *Life* magazine, May 11, 1962.

Barry, Joseph. "Audrey Hepburn at 40" *McCall's*, July 1969.

Bocca, Geoffrey. "The Private World of Audrey Hepburn and Mel Ferrer," *Redbook*, July 1956.

Brunner, Jeryl. "Lookback," *InStyle,* October 2001.

Clement, Carl. "Look Where You're Going, Audrey," *Photoplay*, June 1957.

"Critics Gaga Over Little Audrey's Gigi," *People Today*, January 16, 1952.

Crowe, Cameron. Interview with Billy Wilder. *The Daily Telegraph*, November 9, 1999.

de Givenchy, Hubert. *Newsweek*. South American edition, July 19, 1999.

Dunn, Angela Fox. "Audrey Hepburn Is a Class Act," *Rochester Democrat and Chronicle*, December 21, 1989.

Dunne, Dominick. "Hepburn Heart," *Vanity Fair*, May 1991.

Fields, Sidney. "Success Is Not Security," *McCalls*, July 1954.

Garcia, Guy D. *Time* magazine, People, April 4, 1988.

Gelder, Henk van. "Hepburns Nederlandse filmdebut," ("Hepburn's Dutch Film Debut"), *NRC Handelsblad*, January 22, 1993, translated by Paul Vroemen.

Gittelson, Natalie. "Audrey Hepburn," *McCalls*, August 1989.

Hamilton, Jack. "Audrey Hepburn and Her Strong Son," *Look* magazine, November 8, 1960.

Hepburn, Audrey. "Where Hope Is Last to Die," *USA Today*, May 26, 1989.

Hepburn, Audrey. "Unforgettable Silence," *Newsweek*, October 26, 1992.

Hermann, Helen Markel. "Half Nymph, Half Wunderkind," *The New York Times Magazine*, February 14, 1954.

Jones, Mary Worthington. "My Husband Doesn't Run Me," *Photoplay*, April 1956.

Judge, D. Audrey. "The New Audrey," *Ladies Home Journal*, January 1976.

Klein, Edward. "One Woman's Search for Love: A Profile of Audrey Hepburn," *Parade*, March 5, 1989.

Lavin, Cheryl. "Vital Statistics—Audrey Hepburn" *St. Louis Post Dispatch*, November 8, 1989.

"Look at Audrey Hepburn," *Ladies Home Journal,* January 1967.

Loos, Anita. "Everything Happens to Audrey Hepburn," *The American Weekly*, September 12, 1954.

Mansfield, Stephanie. "Audrey Hepburn, Eternal Waif," *New York Post*, August 31, 1985.

Maynard, John. "Audrey's Harvest of the Heart," *Photoplay*, September 1956.

"People Column," *St. Louis Post-Dispatch*, April 24, 1991.

People Extra: A Tribute to Audrey Hepburn, Winter, 1993.

Pepper, Curtis Bill. "The Return of Audrey Hepburn," *McCall's*, January 1976.

Pepper, Curtis Bill. "The Loving World of Audrey Hepburn Dotti," *Vogue*, April 1971.

Plaskin, Glenn. "She Hardly Goes Lightly Through Life," *Richmond News Leader*, May 24, 1991.

Plaskin, Glenn. "Audrey Hepburn," *US Weekly*, October 17, 1988.

Podolsky, J.D. "Life with Audrey Hepburn," *Who Weekly*, November 14, 1994.

Press, Robert M. "A Visit of Compassion to Somalia," *Christian Science Monitor*, October 5, 1992.

Reed, Rex. "Our Fair Lady Is Back, and It's Spring," *New York Sunday News*, March 21, 1976.

Riding, Alan. *The New York Times* Paris bureau, interview with Audrey Hepburn, April 12, 1991.

Riding, Alan. "Lincoln Center Honors Audrey Hepburn," *St. Paul Pioneer Press*, April 23, 1991.

Ringel, Eleanor. "Audrey Hepburn Is Leading Lady for World's Kids," *The Atlanta Constitution*, March 2, 1991.

Schindehette, Susan (et. al.). "Our Fair Lady," *Who Weekly*, February 1, 1993.

Seidenbaum, Art. *"Audrey Hepburn: Making of My Fair Lady,"* McCalls, *October 1964.*

"Stars Who Danced," *The Saturday Review*, November 15, 1952.

Swanson, Pauline. "Knee-Deep in Stardust," *Photoplay*, April 1954.

Time magazine, "Princess Apparent," September 7, 1953.

Vincent, Mal. "To Movie-Goers, Audrey Hepburn Will Always Be 'My Fair Lady,'" *Norfolk Virginian-Pilot*, February 22, 1987.

Waters, Jim. "The Voice, the Neck, the Charm: They Just Don't Make Movie Stars Like Audrey Hepburn Anymore," *People* magazine, April 12, 1976.

Woolridge, Jane. "At This Stage of Her Life, Hepburn's Still a Fair Lady," *The Miami Herald*, December 3, 1989.

Wuntch, Phillip. "Audrey Hepburn Reminisces," *The Dallas Morning News*, March 2, 1991.

Bibliography

Fox, Patty. *Star Style: Hollywood Legends as Fashion Icons* (Angel City Press: Hong Kong, 1995).

Giles, Sarah. *Fred Astaire: His Friends Talk* (New York: Random House Value Publishing, 1990).

Harris, Warren G. "Audrey Hepburn—A Biography" (Wheeler Publishing, Inc./Simon & Schuster 1994).

Higham, Charles. *Audrey. The Life of Audrey Hepburn* (New York: Macmillan Publishing Company, 1985).

Hofstede, David. *Audrey Hepburn: A Bio-Bibliography* (Greenwood: Green Press, 1994).

Karney Robyn. *A Star Danced: The Life of Audrey Hepburn* (Bloomsbury Publishing Limited, 1993).

Keogh, Pamela Clarke. *Audrey Style* (New York: HarperCollins, 1999).

Morley, Sheridan. *Audrey Hepburn: A Celebration* (London: Pavilion Books Limited, 1993),

Paris, Barry. *Audrey Hepburn* (New York: G.P. Putnam's Sons, 1996).

Ricci, Stefania. *Audrey Hepburn* (Museo Salvatore Ferragamo/Leonardo Arte, 1999).

Silverman, Steven M. *Dancing on the Ceiling: Stanley Donen and His Movies,* introduction by Audrey Hepburn (New York: Knopf, 1996).

Woodward, Ian. *Audrey Hepburn* (London: Virgin Books, 1993)

Walker, Alexander. *Audrey: Her Real Story* (Weidenfeld & Nicolson, 1994).
Willoughby, Bob. *Audrey: An Intimate Collection* (London: Vision On
     Publishing, 2002).

Audio

AH to Terry Gross. *Fresh Air on Stage and Screen with Terry Gross*. 1998.
     (Interview date: 1996).

Video

AH video interview with Bill Collins, Australia, 1989.
AH interview on *Donahue*, host Phil Donahue, January 31, 1990.
AH interview with Shara Fryer, KTRK-TV Houston, March 22–23, 1990.
AH interview with Bryant Gumbel, *Today*, September 29, 1992.
"Audrey Hepburn—A Repeat Interview" *Larry King Live* (CNN), host
     Larry King, June 24, 1995.
AH interview with Barbara Walters, March 29, 1989.
Audrey Hepburn Remembered, narrated by Roger Moore, Wombat
     Productions, Gene Feldman, producer, 1993.
Audrey Hepburn: The Fairest Lady, A & E Entertainment, 1998; Twentieth
     Century Fox Film Corporation, Kevin Burns, executive producer, 1997.
Gardens of the World with Audrey Hepburn, Julie Leifermann, producer,
     Perennial Productions, 1993.
Great Romances of the 20th Century: Audrey Hepburn and Mel Ferrer.
     Women's Entertainment Television (WE).
Lifetime's Intimate Portrait: Audrey Hepburn, with host Meredith Viera,
     Linda Ellman, executive producer, Lifetime Television.

Other

AH statement to the UN staff at "The 1% for Development Fund" meeting,
     Geneva, June 13, 1989.
AH at George Eastman house, Rochester, New York, October 25, 1992.
AH acceptance speech for Screen Actor's Guild Achievement Award, read by
     Julia Roberts, January 10, 1993.
Somalia: The Silent Children, October 1992, Audrey Hepburn. Christopher
     Dickey transcript of one-half-hour discussion for *International
     Newsweek.*

PHOTO CREDITS

Cover: John Engstead/Paramount/ The Kobal Collection

pp. ii–iii: Douglas Kirkland / Corbis

p. xii: Philippe Halsman / Magnum Photos

p. 4: Bob Willoughby / MPTV.net

p. 9: Bettmann / Corbis

p. 12: Cat's / Corbis Sygma

p. 13: The Kobal Collection

p. 15: Popperfoto.com / CPL

p. 16: Philippe Halsman / Magnum Photos

p. 18: John Springer Collection / Corbis

p. 21: David Seymour / Magnum Photos

p. 22: Sanford Roth / MPTV.net

p. 26: David Seymour / Magnum Photos

p. 31: Bettmann / Corbis

p. 33: Dennis Stock / Magnum Photos

p. 34: Bettmann / Corbis

p. 37: Dennis Stock / Magnum Photos

p. 39: Leonard McCombe / Time Life Pictures / Getty Images

p. 40: Bettmann / Corbis

p. 43: MPTV.net

p. 45: MPTV.net

p. 46: MPTV.net

p. 50: Time Life Pictures / Getty Images

p. 53: Mark Shaw / MPTV.net

p. 54: Dennis Stock / Magnum Photos

p. 58: Dennis Stock / Magnum Photos

p. 60: Bob Willoughby / MPTV.net

p. 62: Bettmann / Corbis

p. 66: Bettmann / Corbis

p. 68: Mark Shaw / MPTV.net

p. 72: Paramount / The Kobal Collection

p. 75: 20th Century Fox / The Kobal Collection

p. 77: Mark Shaw / MPTV.net

p. 80 : Bettmann / Corbis

p. 83: MPTV.net

p. 87: Conde Nast Archive / Corbis

p. 88: Hulton Archive / Getty Images

p. 92: Bettmann / Corbis

p. 97: Bettmann / Corbis

p. 101: Bettmann / Corbis

p. 102: Paramount / The Kobal Collection

p. 106: MPTV.net

p. 112: MPTV.net

p. 114: Paramount / The Kobal Collection

p. 117: Photo B.D.V. / Corbis

p. 118: John Swope Trust / MPTV.net

p. 122: Popperfoto.com / CPL

p. 125: Sanford Roth / MPTV.net

p. 127: Norman Parkinson / Corbis Sygma

p. 129: Bettmann / Corbis

p. 132: Mark Shaw / MPTV.net

p. 135: Bob Willoughby / MPTV.net

p. 138: MPTV.net

p. 140: Norman Parkinson / Corbis Sygma

p. 142: Douglas Kirkland / Corbis

p. 145: The Kobal Collection

p. 149: Time Life Pictures / Getty Images

p. 152: Bill Avery / MPTV.net

p. 154: Bettmann / Corbis

p. 157: Bettmann / Corbis

p. 158: Bob Willoughby / MPTV.net

p. 160: Bettmann / Corbis

p. 164: Bettmann / Corbis

p. 168: Paramount / The Kobal Collection

p. 172: Bettmann / Corbis

p. 176: Getty Images

p. 181: Time Life Pictures / Getty Images

p. 184: Robert Wolders / Corbis

p. 188: Derek Hudson / Corbis